QUESTIONS, CHRIST AND THE QUARTER-LIFE CRISIS

SOMETIMES IT TAKES GETTING LOST TO DISCOVER WHO AND WHOSE WE ARE.

MORGAN RICHARD OLIVIER

Lincross Publishing

MORGAN RICHARD OLIVIER

QUESTIONS, CHRIST AND THE QUARTER-LIFE CRISIS

Cover Design by Alex Lewis, Concise Consuting Agency
Interior Design by Lance Butler, Concise Consulting Agency
ISBN: 978-1-948581-74-5

First Edition: May 2020

To my husband, Rusty, for loving me
through my lessons and supporting me
every step of the way

CONTENTS

PART IV: HEALING AND HONORING YOURSELF

PART V: ALL THINGS WORK TOGETHER

MORGAN RICHARD OLIVIER

The journey of self is far more
than realizing who we are.
It's releasing the idea and pressure
of who we and the world
believes we ought to be.

- Morgan Richard Olivier

INTRODUCTION

When I was presented with the opportunity to publish this book, I must admit that I was amazed and terrified at the same time. I experienced a range of emotions not only because writing a book gave me the opportunity to spread my message on a larger scale, but also because expressing my experiences and raw emotions puts me in a vulnerable position—a position to be judged, mocked, and rejected.

For much of my life, any opportunity that presented those three possibilities were ixnayed immediately without hesitation. However, in this season of my life, I wholeheartedly welcome vulnerability. I know that fear and worst-case scenarios will not cloud my mind or hinder my judgment. Though, in seasons of stillness, I endured difficulty and frustration. Now, I reap wisdom that cannot be silenced. It is my season to walk boldly and gracefully in my story of confusion, conversion, and obedience.

For over two years, it has been on my heart and in my spirit to write this book, call it by this very name, and to release the testimonies that are intertwined within these pages. Each of the chapters are rooted in my innermost thoughts. They are reflections from counseling sessions, revelations, and examinations of conscience. What was once a means of coping that was tucked away within the notes of my phone and safe in a desktop document now serves as a torch of wisdom and a resource of hope. It is a testament to my transformation.

I chose to go back in time to copy and paste my inner chaos that, at one time, seemed to overcome my life. This book serves as a life jacket for readers and an anchor for myself, to show how deep I had sunk and how far I have come with psychological help, self-assessments, and the love of God in my life. I am a firm believer and true example that our crises, chaos, and seasons of sheer confusion are not only about the destruction we create, the depression we endure, or the foolish decisions we make. They are about searching ourselves and understanding the *why*, repenting of our wretched ways, fostering growth from every lesson, and loving God and ourselves along the way.

Five years ago, I made my passion public and began writing for a well-known writing community. Though it was something I had never done before, I felt drawn to the opportunity and immediately grew fascinated with the process of writing. However, it was the nature of sharing that captivated me even more. I wrote strictly about the positive stuff: self-love, beauty, and all of the motivational mumbo jumbo. I gave my views on relationships, advice on how to "crush it" in life, and always went out of my way to leave my readers feeling more empowered than when they began reading.

I absolutely loved how expressing my words, thoughts, and emotions not only made me feel, but also how my words affected my audience. I was able to surpass the boundaries of age, race, and even economic status through my words. I was able to encourage them to feel good, one post at a time. Like any 23-year-old, I wrote based on my level of experience and my current season in life. Although writing became a huge part of my life, I felt no desire to showcase God in any of it. Don't get me wrong; I prayed, respected, and loved God. I even occasionally went to church, but I did not feel the need or have the time to get all wrapped up in religion.

In my younger years, I attended Catholic schools. I thought I knew every story in the Bible. I believed that I knew Jesus, and I knew how to get into Heaven. I was nice, had a genuinely good heart, and a great personality. I always made it my purpose to treat others well and held kindness in high regard. I went out of my way to do good, and I worked hard to be the person I thought I should be. I loved God. After all, those were the prerequisites to being a good Christian, right? I thought I was right on track.

In my mind, I was in complete control of my life. My sacrifices, hard work, and dedication had gotten me this far. Of course, I loved God, but what did I need to call on Him for? Why did I need to go to church? I was doing great on my own, or so I thought. However, life taught me otherwise. Low points and losses proved to me that if I didn't have the relationship with The One who created me, then I was opening up my life, my future, and my spirit to the one who can ultimately destroy me. With that being said, the person who stands today is a product of the person I once was. I am the person—who through trial and error, consequences and chastisement, grace and mercy—found her way and can now give glory without shame.

Many born-again Christians like myself share a common thread in our testimonies. Before this version of ourselves could exist, the voice of our egos, the desires of the flesh, and the plans that we had for our lives had to essentially die. Pride, projection, and personas have a way of coming before our falls because, behind each one of them, there is a deeper issue. We fight tirelessly for the win, we compare every bit of our lives to that of social media, and we wallow in the depression of our souls. We usually do not understand humility or faith until we fall flat on our faces. In the eyes of our self-made tornados, we stand in confusion and terror of what has become of the situation.

That, my friends, is where our faith walk begins and the journey to discovering and accepting our authentic selves takes form. The whirlwind of our self-made chaos, though numbing and beyond difficult to navigate, is the perfect ingredient to get us on the right track. This route may not have been on our original plan, but it is the path of wisdom, growth, and purpose that will get us to who we've been created to be.

HOW DID I FIND GOD?

I didn't find God at all. He never hid from me, ignored my calls, or pretended that I didn't exist. That's what I did to Him. Therefore, I didn't find God. I returned to Him. I would love to say I found God on the mountaintops, at the highest point in my career, in the greatest season of my marriage, or at the cusp of something amazing, but that would be a lie. I found God in the season that I completely lost myself, my direction, and my will to live. I called for God whenever I felt I had no one and nothing in my corner. He not only listened, but also spoke to me, carried me, and healed me in ways that I couldn't ignore or forget. He saved me from myself and—because of that— I can't stay silent, wear a mask, or downplay all the destruction that He used to develop me. I have to start where my spiritual blindness ended.

My 25th year of life changed everything for me. It was the year that started with me on top of the world and ended with the weight of the world on my shoulders. My direction in life seemed nonexistent, my mental and physical health plummeted, my marriage struggled tremendously, my grandparents passed away, and my faith was created and tested simultaneously. To say Chapter 25 of my life was an eye opener is an understatement. It was a year of soul-breaking and soul-searching. It was the year I learned the most about the world, my surroundings, my life, God, and myself. It was my catalyst.

Every lesson learned, tear cried, and prayer prayed was used for a bigger purpose. My imperfections made me perfect for my purpose and gave me the grace to write this book. I say that because as young people, we look to our twenties as our years to truly live life. We venture out, go to college, pursue careers, find our spouse, and live happily ever after. We plan the trips that we are going to take and the memories along the way. The world is at our fingertips, and the future is in our hands. However, knowing now what I didn't know then, our twenties are seldom the very best times of our lives. Oftentimes, our twenties are our chapters of trial and error. They are the years of our lives when we try to do things on our own and sometimes find ourselves failing. They are when we learn the value of a dollar and see the value of hard work. Our twenties open us up to experiences that we never had before, align us with people who we didn't even know existed, and allow us to look at the world through a whole new lens. We compare connections with conditions and truly begin to question ourselves, our lives, and everything in it. It is an amazing yet uncomfortable time for many of us. It is a rude awakening that has the power to align us with our spiritual awakening. It is essentially where our story and journey of self truly begins.

Millions of people are in the midst of this season and are walking in this transformation, yet many of us allow the world to tell our story. We allow the lessons that were so loud to be silently swept under the rug. We allow our enemies to take paint a portrait that misconstrues us but catches the eye of comparison. We let our past dictate and suppress our new and improved self. We allow our real testimonies—the stories of our redemption, redirection, and revelation—to go unheard.

Well, I choose to be vocal. I choose to be vulnerable and talk about victory. I choose to walk in grace and give glory along the way. Pain, problems, and low points did not destroy me. I did not crumble in what psychology may call my "Quarter-life Crisis." I was created in it. This happened—because through the questions, through my confusion, through my qualms, through the chaos, and through my cries—I called on Christ.

PART I

PRESSURE,
PAIN AND
PROBLEMS

You've gone through a multitude of phases in life, phases where you believed you knew it all and phases where you felt you knew absolutely nothing. You've been through phases where you experienced consecutive wins and phases where you felt you couldn't keep your head above water. Out of the phases experienced and faced, it is the phase of not knowing or understanding yourself and your life that terrifies you the most. It's realizing that no person can step in and save all of your days. It's recognizing that the life you prayed for, expected, and worked so hard to obtain may not be what you need. In the midst of struggling to understand who you are and where you are going, you reach a destination where you know you don't want to be.

- Morgan Richard Olivier

CHAPTER 1
WHAT'S GOING ON?

With tears dripping off of my face to my bare chest and my greasy hair wrapped in a bun, I was sulked in complete numbness. I can vividly remember locking myself in my bathroom, sitting in my bathtub, and smelling the scent of lavender bath salts and sweat seeping through every pore. While adding hot water to my overdrawn bath, I kept the song "What's Up" by 4 Non Blondes on repeat. I was drained, damaged, and felt like I was slowly and painfully dying. I couldn't help but feel stagnant, helpless, and hopeless. Just like the song, I couldn't figure out for the life of me what was going on. Every time I felt I was taking one step forward, I was simultaneously taking seven steps back. Every time I placed my finger on the problem and inched toward healing, it seemed like more problems, emotions, and obstacles would be revealed. Nothing in my life was right. Everything I had worked for seemed worthless and void. The beautiful house I lived in felt more like a prison than a place of comfort. No matter how many heels I had in my walk-in closet, not one could make me get out of bed and face the day. Not even the most beautiful window could inspire me to take in the warmth of the sun. I would not open my curtains. I was a prisoner in my own home, a slave to the world, and my own worst enemy. Even though I didn't realize it at the time, I couldn't overcome the war zone that existed in my mind.

I was going to church, earnestly and actively working on myself, and doing everything I was supposed to do. Why was I at war? Why was this happening to me? Would there ever be an end to this misery? Would I ever be happy again?

As I looked in the mirror, I could hardly recognize myself. I was down 18 pounds, and the bones in my face were showing. My eyes were empty and puffed from the amount of tears I had been crying.

I didn't know her. I didn't know the girl in the mirror. Where was the person I once knew? Where was the one with bright eyes, a bubbly personality, and full face who always tried to be positive? Where was the girl whose laugh was just as goofy as her corny jokes, the one who naturally smiled with every word she spoke? Did I ever know her, or was she just a projection of my imagination? I stood there looking at a shell. I didn't know anything about her. I didn't know her hobbies, talents, dislikes, passions, or weaknesses. I didn't know her *secret power* or that thing that made her unique. I didn't see that strong person and friend who everyone else saw. I saw a mask that had finally come off and a young, ignorant person was completely lost, standing there behind it.

My reflection allowed me to see who I was not. My awareness was the floodgate that allowed me to feel again. My life was falling apart, and I could not pick up the pieces. I had no idea who I was, but I knew what I was not.

CAN'T RUN FROM MYSELF

When problems arise, hardships take over, or we experience loss, the very first thing many of us desperately want to do is distance ourselves from it. Whatever "it" is, it's a threat to our safety, comfort, or lives. Sometimes, it's a combination of all three. We don't want to feel the pain, the suffering, or the depression. Don't look at it, and don't touch it. Definitely, don't talk about it. It's an open sore. We just want it to go away, and if it can't, then we will. We come up with a plethora of elaborate and calculated ways we can just remove ourselves from whatever or whoever we don't want to accept. In our minds, fleeing seems like a more rational and acceptable solution than fighting something right in front of us.

We flee from many things for a multitude of reasons, and no matter if the issue is on the relationship, career, health, or social aspect of our lives, we somehow always find a way to resort to running as a means to an end.

Example One:

The relationship spark seems to have fizzled out and loneliness has crept in where compliments and companionship used to be. Maybe if we leave our boyfriend/girlfriend or husband/wife, then we can find someone who not only appreciates and compliments us more, but also is a better fit for the life we've come to fantasize.

Example Two:

No one in our hometowns can see beyond our pasts or the rumors associated with them. If we move away and get settled in new environments, then we can start fresh and finally move forward. We can be who we always wanted to be and have better control of our destinies.

As great as all of that may sound, that way of thinking and addressing issues is not realistic or ultimately beneficial. Unfortunately, it's usually whenever we begin running from problems, pains, and people that we simultaneously run into new issues and repeat a revised version of a cycle that just won't seem to end.

RUNNING TO TRANSFORMATION

I was tired. Months prior, I updated my resume' and thought I needed a new job or something different in my life, but now I was completely certain that I wanted and needed a fresh start. I thought about changing my look, moving away, opening a new office, and even returning to school. I figured the only way to a fresh start was starting anew. I would be happy. I wasn't running away; I was trying to live a new and improved life, a life I actually wanted to live. I was going to create a life that I was in complete control of.

I wanted a fresh start, so I took action. I traveled to Louisville, Kentucky, and scouted neighborhoods and prospective employment opportunities with my husband. I wasted no time. I was on my "A" game. I was going to take the family business to new heights in a place that already had the foundation and a business presence. I had this *pack up everything and go* mindset where I was perfectly fine with leaving everything and everyone behind. As time progressed and Hindsight worked her magic, I began to see my motives for a move. I was running from my life. The more I tried to run, hide, and shield myself from the mental, physical, spiritual, and environmental pain that I was experiencing, the more I prolonged it. Every avenue that I thought would work as a shortcut only made the journey to healing more difficult to navigate. Running became a style of living, and it was hurting me. Before I knew it, I was drowning, held down, and enslaved to it.

The more I sat and reflected, the more apparent my pattern became. I wasn't being productive. I was being reactive. I was running just like I had always done. I realized that flight was simply my response of choice and that was why, internally, I was fighting so many things. I wasn't fighting for a fresh start; I was fighting to flee every situation without learning the depths of these tough life lessons. I was trying to distance myself from discomfort.

I could dye my hair, change my name, get a new job, move across the world and start over, but truly nothing would ever change. No matter how far or fast I ran, I would always be there. I would always be held captive by my own fears. It is no wonder why I was drained and tired. I was unable to stand still and learn what was ahead of me.

The thing about pain is that it is not only important to acknowledge it, but it's critical that we take steps back and try to understand why it exists in the first place. Pain isn't allowed simply with the sole intention to hurt. Pain is a great teacher, and if we make the choice to learn from it, then it can act as our greatest precursor to growth. Therefore, if pain won't seem to leave, the question isn't, *why me?* The question should be, *what is this pain trying to teach me?*

Running from my fears was not the solution; facing them head on was. My fears were not attached to people, situations, or my setting. My fear was within me. I had to face and detoxify my mind and spirit. It was time to run to the roots of my problems and identify how and why this season existed.

I have everything, yet I feel nothing at all.

- Morgan Richard Olivier

CHAPTER 2
EMPTINESS

I can vividly remember the morning of September 23, 2016, and waking up to gold and black helium filled balloons everywhere with the golden number 25. I was officially a "Quarter Century Old," as my friends would say, and I could not hide my excitement. A new chapter in my life had begun. My husband, Rusty, completely outdid himself. From the huge cookie cake and the countless balloons to the fun dinner and game night with friends, it was a memorable day.

My 25th year of life started off with a bang. In fact, I can still hear the echo of my words that night. I told everyone that something big was going to happen in my 25th year. I didn't know what it was, but I could feel it in my bones. This year was going to be different from the rest. This would be my year, and, in many ways, it was. It was the year that changed everything.

At 25 years old, I entered a season where it felt as though I had everything but nothing at all. On paper, I was in a position that most women my age would dream about. I was married to my high school sweetheart, had a great job, owned a beautiful home, and was very well-liked. I was gaining popularity for my *self-love* writing, so much so, that it gained national attention. I was constantly building momentum in the business and appeared to be winning every time I turned around. I was on fire, and people noticed. I was finally at that level of perfection I always strived for.

On the exterior, I was experiencing a high, and I documented all of it. It was a social media dream come true. There was just one underlying problem. I didn't want to be the perfect person anymore. I didn't want to be the person who had to do and say what everyone wanted her to. Of course, all of my friends, family and coworkers loved that, but it left me empty, agitated, and inquisitive. I had so much going for me and so much to show for it, but no matter how much was around me and how much praise I was getting, there was always an overwhelming, underlying feeling of emptiness that silently followed me like a dark cloud. There was a void that I could never seem to accurately fill. I felt like a caged bird who was safe and secure yet agitated and longing for freedom. I was a beautiful and entertaining bird who would sing and mimic whatever the crowd wanted, but, as soon as they'd turn away, I would find myself banging my head against the cage.

The more I thought about it, the angrier I became. I wanted freedom but could not find an escape. My yes to everything and everyone fulfilled everyone but me. I was saying no to opportunities and activities that I always wanted to try, not because I was told I couldn't, but because I had preconceived notions of who I thought others wanted me to be. In my heart and mind, I had to live up to my image and "stay in my lane" where everything was safe. It was something I had done my entire life.

As long as I could remember, I was Type A and known for being the good girl. I never got in trouble, really didn't have enemies, and lived a sheltered, safe life. I lived for and by the rules. I always had the desire to be a good person and worked to be great. Whether it was excelling in high school or graduating college summa cum laude, I always wanted to be recognized and known for my good works. I strived to be the smart, accomplished woman and made sure my life went in line with just that.

I never went to high school parties and definitely never even thought about attending any college activities. I was too scared of how others would view me. I seldom tried new things and always stuck to what I knew. Even after getting my degree, my life was confined to what I'd known my entire life: my husband, the family business, and my list of goals. That was always it, and I was always happy because that was more than enough for me. However, as I began questioning my surroundings and myself, I felt there was more to life than what I had already lived.

The world that I once feared became oddly fascinating whenever I felt I was not stimulated or happy enough. What else is out there? What if I'm not even supposed to be in this line of work? What if my life is just a consequence of my comfort? Maybe there is more to life. There has to be more to life than the routine, hidden resentments, and rush to complete the next goal.

THE SEA OF QUESTIONS

We have the things we always wanted in life and worked so hard to gain. Now, what do we do? What do we do from this point? Do we make a new goal or appreciate every season and lesson that mounted up to this chapter in our lives? No, instead, we critique and question an assortment of things.

What am I doing with my life? There has to be something that I'm missing. Where is all of this coming from? Is the life I'm living the one I'm destined to fulfill? Am I playing a part or practicing what I really want to do?

Career

Yes, I have my dream job that came from the degree I worked so hard to earn, but do I actually enjoy this type of work? Can I see myself doing this for the rest of my life? Did I choose a major because the future job would offer me a lot of money or because it was going to be an easy four years of college to endure? Did I even go to college for myself?

Marriage

Where do I go from here? What goal should I accomplish now, so that my life can be interesting? Yes, I have a great husband/wife, but did we make the choice too soon or too young? Did I travel, experience, or search myself enough before I became one with my spouse? Does this person love me? Are we comfortable or compatible with each other?

Family

Did I have children too young? I could only imagine how much more successful and ahead in life I would be if I didn't have the responsibility of another person. Did I ruin my adult life before it truly even had a chance to start?

Life

Is my life simply an accumulation of my goals or something that I actually desire? What if this isn't even the life I should be living? What if I need to move? What if that's the reason I don't feel happy or whole? What if I'm not living my best life?

We shouldn't question these things, yet we can't stop.

THE CRAVING

We analyze every aspect of our lives. We find ourselves either in the realm of too much or not enough, defined by the approval of others and constantly being fed ideals of what our lives are supposed to be. We don't have enough money in the bank, shoes to keep up with the trends, or outfits that made us feel empowered or look the part. We don't have enough friends on Facebook, followers on Instagram, or retweets on Twitter. Our jobs don't challenge us. Our families do not understand or appreciate us. Nothing feels right or in balance. We begin to convince ourselves that we are going through the motions of a mediocre life, and something must be done. All of a sudden, we aren't traveling enough, and our features aren't toned enough. The people around us simply don't do it for us anymore. We need to get married, get divorced, have children, or do whatever it is that we're not doing. We need to do interesting things and document everything to share on social media. We need something.

We need change, so we should get to it. We need something that stimulates our minds and makes our hearts beat just a little faster. We need to find a way to live our best lives, even if it means it will cost us the comfort, stability, and practicality of our current ones. We crave an adrenaline rush or something that will make us feel like we are finally doing something or considered someone. Life is short, and we only live once. Let's do it. What's the worst that can happen, right? That's where it all starts to fall apart, in a slow, seemingly unrecognizable fashion.

It was the feeling of wanting and needing more that made me enjoy and appreciate my life less. At some point, the amount of friends, compliments, accomplishments, and validations could not outweigh the burdens on my shoulders or fill that void in my heart. I had everything I ever wanted, yet I felt empty. I felt like I was going with the motions of life, smiling through, and showing up, but I reached a point that I was no longer getting anything out of it. I was just there.

There was this void that hung over me like a dark cloud that I couldn't seem to figure out or fill, and everything I tried to stuff it with only brought me more stress, confusion, and despair. I looked to pills to heal the pain, people to say what I wanted to hear, accomplishments to validate my worth, profits to afford me items that would warrant temporary happiness, and overcompensation to fool myself and the world into believing that I was happy and content, but I was the farthest thing from it. I was struggling, and I was drowning, but from the outside looking in, I was perfect. I cried multiple times a day: in the car on the way to work, as I took my long exercise walks, and in the shower. That's when I really let my emotions loose. In my mind, that was normal. That's healthy, right? Everyone cries from time to time.

What makes me any different? That level of confusion was not good for me, at all.

I was desperately looking for something that completed me, but that thing was unknown to me. I craved it, cried for it, and yearned for it, but I didn't know what it was. I didn't know what it looked like, smelled like, tasted like, sounded like, or how it felt. Was it money, a job, a person, a child, a position, or even a tangible thing? It seemed like I was losing it all, looking for something that couldn't be described or identified by one of my five senses. One thing was sure. I wasn't whole without it. This void, though not seen to the eye, felt as though it created a gaping hole in the center of my chest and in the center of my life. I couldn't ignore it, even if I tried.

I needed and searched for more, but as time went on, it was never enough. The more attention I got, the more I needed. The more money I made, the more ways I needed to find to make more. The more friends I had, the more I needed to please them, so they would hold me in high regard. If I had something, I needed more of it. I needed it to bring me happiness, and if it didn't bring me happiness, the least it could do was bring me some form of approval.

LONGING AND BELONGING

I often found myself discouraged, upset, and even enraged whenever I felt like no one understood or could actually relate to me. I had to speak in a way and at a level that was easily understood by the masses but didn't even touch the surface of how I intended to adequately express myself. I craved conversations that were so stimulating that they'd require me to analyze the depths of my mind, soul, education, and life experiences. I wanted to see and learn about things that I previously didn't know existed. I wanted to go places and be exposed to unique cultures and unconventional ways of thinking. Being deemed as intelligent wasn't enough. My inquisitive and ignorant worldly eyes wanted to explore and experiment. Some call that rebellious; others may view it as reckless. All I wanted to do was experience something real. I did not want to be overprotected by my family or to be a puppet on a string for my friends. I wanted to do something for myself, for once.

I began to feel like I was drowning in a life that I worked so hard to create for myself, a life that everyone seemed to want but me. Everything I had worked toward and cared about seemed to be detaching from me, and it wasn't long before my connection to my reality seemed to wander with it. I felt a range of bubbling up emotions and felt each one so deeply.

I was no longer content or satisfied with this version of myself. I craved more. I needed to see more, try more, and be more than I had ever been. For a usually reserved person, I got this intense drive to see myself shine and break out of the shell in which I always resided. After all, it seemed like every time I turned around, people were telling me to try this, go there, dress like this, and be like that. Why not reach for what everyone was saying? If they see more for me, then shouldn't I? I have what it takes: the drive, capacity, and passion to achieve more. I have my hand in a multitude of projects, sit on several boards, and am succeeding in all my endeavors, but I still do not feel content. I still feel stagnant and that this can't be it for me.

Though my ego seemed to be my source, my self-esteem started to plummet. It was the latter part of 2016 that I started feeling very off, very empty, and very overwhelmed. I began experiencing bouts of depression, feeling lost in the world, alone amongst the people who were supposed to know me best, and trapped within the version of myself that I had created. I felt taken advantage of, overlooked, and undervalued in many aspects of my life. I felt like I was putting on a show.

BEHIND THE MASK

Oh, how looks can be deceiving, how pain can be polished into making anyone appear like they have the perfect life, and how even blessings can be disregarded by those who are spiritually and emotionally blind. Emptiness and loneliness are very interesting yet misunderstood crosses that many of us will carry throughout different seasons of our lives. Though their entrances into our lives seem to be without a sound, their impacts on our mentalities, relationships, and lives speak volumes.

It comes in waves, at first. Something just doesn't feel right. We don't understand, yet we don't question the emotions. We simply move past them and believe that it's all in our heads. Those feelings of being out of place and somewhat of an outcast are quickly followed up by our own positive reassurance. We tell ourselves that we are being overdramatic or that we're thinking too much into our own situations or feelings. As time progresses, what was once easy to compartmentalize seems too pressing to ignore and too complicated to uncover or explain. We cover up our loneliness, fear of rejection, and insecurities with fake smiles, loud laughs, and social media posts that make it appear that we are living and loving our best life. We convince the world that we are okay because, deep down inside, it's easier for us to try to ignore the fact that we are not.

CRY FOR HELP

It is so difficult to express why we are sad, why we are lost, why we are confused, why we are empty or why we are angry, whenever we don't truly know ourselves. How do we articulate why we are making the wrong decisions everywhere we turn, why we feel trapped behind a facade of who we are expected to be, why we can't tell up from down, and why whenever we stare at ourselves, we see nothing familiar?

The problem that most of us have is that we are trying to make others understand the depths of our confusion in the very same seasons that we are most confused. Those are not times to explain ourselves to people or try to get them to side with us or understand us. Those are the times in our lives where we are trying with everything in us to figure it out.

All my life, I felt like I had to hold my tongue for everything. Speaking or standing up for how I felt was not an option. I avoided defending myself or rocking the boat and often found myself taken advantage of. I kept my mouth shut and a smile on because the only thing I hated more than the feeling of being ignored or misunderstood was the fear and tension that stemmed from confrontation. I purposely chose to not fight battles with anyone or anything around me and wound up creating war within myself. I found myself angry at the world and a prisoner of it.

It was exhausting to feel but even more exhausting to keep up the facade. Before long, I couldn't take it anymore. I started getting what people would likely call *mood swings*. I began experiencing times of aggravation that stemmed from resentments and the suppression of my feelings. It got to the point that I had to say something.

However, when I was crying, pleading, and reaching out, I felt that no one seemed to care. Whenever I wanted to express myself, no one wanted to listen. I was a good friend, spouse, and family member. Couldn't everyone just be there for me as I was there for them? Was that too much to ask? Why should I continue to suffer in silence? It was time to use my voice, right? Even a strong friend deserves a helping hand. I shouldn't feel like this is a crime. I had hit a wall. No matter how many times I tried to spell it out, it wouldn't change the fact that they couldn't read my words, my emotions, my efforts, or my pain. Very few people seemed to understand, help, or care for what I was enduring.

It was clear that some people were truly concerned, while others simply entertained me for their own sake or to fill their conscience with the typical, "I tried." I knew they were saying things to make me feel better, but that would be the extent of their care or concern. Maybe it was all a part of my imagination, but I felt alone, misunderstood, and bewildered in every way. Quite honestly, the fact that those closest to me were okay with me not being okay was a problem. I was angry with the lack of empathy and unhelpful responses I received.

COMMON PICK-ME-UPS

"You're a strong person. You'll get through this."

"You're a smart girl; you'll figure it out."

"I felt like that before. You'll survive."

"You are overthinking and oversensitive. Everything is going to be fine."

Those one-liners were the farthest thing from encouragement to me. Telling me that I was going to be okay was not okay, in my eyes. They were general go-to phrases to get someone out of a funk or to stop feeling sorry for themselves, and it felt like a slap in the face. I didn't just want to communicate my feelings. I so badly wanted them to be comprehended. I wanted someone to give me sound advice and show me the way. If I couldn't get that, I at least wanted to feel like I wasn't invisible.

I was well aware that life continued for others, but a minute of perceived concern and care would have made all the difference. A little more conversation would have been comforting. Therefore, I stopped crying and trying to explain myself to *my people* and instead I spoke to anyone who would listen. I thought what I needed was direction. I needed a manual or someone to tell me how to and what to do. I looked for guidance. I searched for answers and expressed my lack of direction to those who I believed could point me in the right direction: therapists, family members, friends, associates, and even strangers. Ironically, directions were provided:

> *"You should try this. You should go here. Get involved in this organization. Go back to school. Try this form of therapy. Say a prayer. Quit your job. Do this. Stop that. Associate with this crowd. Your life would be better if you had this. I can help you."*

I heard it all.

Everyone seemed to have a solution to my problem, and every solution seemed so easily believable and adoptable to me. Every piece of advice seemed so profound. Every problem they claimed to have solved felt resolved to me. Why wouldn't I take their advice? They wouldn't lead me in the wrong direction. They know better than I do. That's what I told myself and truly believed. Everyone knew what was best for me, at the time.

Unfortunately, that foolish thinking and naive outlook was far from correct and led me down a path that not only changed the course of that season but also changed the course of my life. My decisions and thought processes became almost polar opposite than normal. I wanted healing, happiness, success, compliments, promotion, and to be the best, and I wanted it now.

I found myself feeling, saying, and going through things that were both out of character and out of my typical comfort zone.

My attempts to fill every void only left me feeling more pain. Eventually, I became a stranger to myself. I could not recognize my thoughts or actions. I was slowly spiraling out of control. Before things got better, they got worse. I kissed a guy that wasn't my husband, and I maxed out my credit card. I tried to numb my chaos with prescriptions and started pushing everyone away. It seemed like every choice I made was wrong, and every way I tried to fix it was worse. I was angry, confused, irrational, and seemingly unpredictable. All of a sudden, the person that always had it together struggled to function.

I couldn't for the life of me understand what was happening. Where was all of this coming from, and why now? I've gotten compliments before, but why do compliments mean so much now? Why do I need people to tell me I'm pretty or intelligent to feel it? Why am I searching for guidance from anyone who is willing to give their opinion? Why do I feel like I'm fighting this inner rage and sadness that comes in waves? How can someone so intelligent be so ignorant, so impressionable, so irresponsible, and so indecisive? I found it so odd that I had always been the type of person who never took medication to fight cold or virus symptoms, yet here I was taking medication from family and friends to treat my anxiety. I never broke any rules or even wanted to, but it was like I was in self-sabotage mode.

I couldn't make sense of it all.

Why am I spending all of this money? I am, by far, the most frugal person I know. Why am I maxing out my credit card? I am usually apprehensive whenever it comes to trying new things, so why am I so impulsive and irresponsible right now? I have a family history of mental illness. Maybe I'm Schizophrenic, Bipolar, or Paranoid. I've already been diagnosed with Anxiety and Depression. Are these signs of another disorder? Maybe it's not a mental illness. Maybe I'm just losing my mind.

I had no idea how I got to that point or how I would get out. The numbness and tears were never ending, and I thought it would never stop. I was experiencing so many emotions at one time that facial expressions and my words were nonexistent. That was the very first time in my life that I was at a complete loss for words.

You know you are lost when you find yourself in situations, emotions, and problems that you never imagined you'd be. You know you are lost when you look at yourself in the mirror and don't even recognize the person who is staring back at you. You know you are lost when you are willing to do and give anything to have your peace, health, and life back in order. It's that mental, physical, emotional, and spiritual place that is both eerily silent yet so uncomfortably loud. What is happening?

The deafening sound of silence and the stench of stagnation fills your home. The tear-soaked tissues fill your bed. The feeling of numbness trickles through your body, and the sadness shakes you to the core. It's a dark cloud that won't seem to go away and a spirit of anguish that attaches to seemingly every aspect of life. As you drown in the depths of depression, you would give all that you have to simply keep your head above water and pray that help of any sort can make a way to you.

- Morgan Richard Olivier

CHAPTER 3
DEPRESSION

There are seasons in life that we will never forget. Milestones such as graduation, the birth of our children, purchasing a home, and getting married leave a warm, fuzzy, and happy feeling in our hearts. They become memories of freedom and lovely points in our lives. But just as the positives are celebrated, the pain and scars of the bad somehow never truly leave. Our past pain is always just a memory and feeling away. We may be able to move past it, but we never truly forget the damage it caused.

These seasons painfully show us the inadequacy of our solutions, the failures that fall upon us, and the trials which replay the downfall of every fiber of our beings. We begin to believe that the prayers we prayed or the prescriptions we took are never really enough. Nothing seems to cure us, and crumbling appears to be the only option. This is because we are not only depressed; we are also drained and distraught.

Looking back, I realize that my depression did not start at 25; it simply progressed and made its grand appearance that year.

For a very long time, I hid my depression behind perfection, accomplishments, and titles. Don't get me wrong; I was extremely blessed beyond measure and naturally very driven. However, I had to be the best at anything I pursued in my life. No matter how much stress it brought, I had to maintain an image of what social media would call #goals. I was "crushing it" in life but struggling to live it.

I just wanted it all to end. I couldn't take another day living behind the persona. I was lost, and I was hurting others because I was hurting. I felt defeated. How could this be? The amount of hate and disdain that I had for myself superseded the idea of a better tomorrow. I was tired of the fake happiness. I was tired of feeling like a puppet on a string. I was tired of existing and didn't see why I even had to continue. If I would die, then everything would stop. The pain would go away; the feelings of failure and rejection would cease to exist. The weight of worrying would be nonexistent. I would be free of it all, and there was nothing that I wanted more.

There was no more singing, no more planning for tomorrow, and no more smiles. There was just pain, confusion, hatred, guilt, shame, embarrassment, and numbness. I came to the realization that my pain had created a completely different version of myself. With each tear that crossed my face, the person I once was slowly washed away. I went from loving to meet new people to keeping my distance and not trusting. I was sensitive, fragile, and upset. I avoided people, places, and things that triggered further discomfort and put my pain on a pedestal.

I reminisced about the dreams I had as a little girl. The dreams which I had worked so hard for, I was now destroying. I no longer understood my place in it. I couldn't explain it to myself and certainly couldn't explain it to anyone else. How did I get to this point? How do you go from feeling like you're on cloud nine to feeling like you will never get out of the pit? My attempts to solve this issue were in vain. No amount of counseling sessions, praying, or advice seemed to work. There was no point in trying. I began questioning if my best course of action was to check myself into a mental institution. I vividly remember researching mental hospitals and verifying if my insurance covered it. I didn't trust myself; my thoughts were driving me crazy. The silence consumed me. Though I was never admitted, I thought of its potential positive benefits often.

I decided it was time to use medication for how I was feeling. I was embarrassed to ask my doctor, but, at this point, I felt only an antidepressant could help me. Although appointments and prescriptions tried to take the edge off, I was still so depressed and disoriented. Ativan, Xanax, and Wellbutrin were supposed to fix me, but it seemed like they only made me worse. I was too impaired to associate with people or drive but sedated enough to function. I went from feeling depressed to feeling suicidal. Every time I closed my eyes, I could see myself walking to an edge and peacefully falling off. I fantasized about it, and I cried about it. I wished it could just stop. Every night, I prayed that I wouldn't wake up the next morning. I just wanted to go peacefully and leave the world behind. I wanted to leave the stress, sadness, and pain behind. However, every morning I found myself waking up in the prison of a bedroom that I set up for myself.

I went from being a person that had to have her house spotless to becoming a recluse who lived in a wreck. I couldn't remember the last time I washed my hair. On certain occasions, I wore the same outfit for at least five days straight. I just gave up. My dirty dishes and smelly laundry became my home's scent. Clearly, my life was out of control. I knew I needed God at that point. I had zero answers, I had tried it all, and nothing had worked. Maybe God could help me make sense out of this mess.

I remembered my younger days in high school and the impact of attending *Life Teen* and Mass. Going to church and simply being in that environment always brought a unique peace to me, back then. I just hoped that stepping into church would help me.

As I began praying and going back to Mass, I started seeing the changes of my mindset and attitude towards life. Every night, I said a prayer. I made it to service every weekend, and I could really feel the impact of the readings. I was giving every Bible verse and message shared with me all of my attention. For that one hour in church, I felt great. I felt safe and uplifted. I felt like everything was going to be okay. In that pew, I had a feeling of peace. Unfortunately, that feeling always faded after I left. It was as if a ton of bricks would fall on me as I left to carry on with my day. There I was, once again, overwhelmed by my anxiety and depression. I wished I could live in church, but I couldn't. Realistically, I couldn't pray the rosary all day either.

I was definitely growing spiritually and mentally, and I was learning to truly receive what was written in the Bible, but I was still hurting and hurting badly. Going to church and being around other believers was good, but I needed more. I needed to not only feel my pain and heal my soul but also needed to find my faith and myself.

Going back to church opened my heart, mind, and eyes to the importance of being right with God and His plan for my life. It revealed to me that depression and anxiety are just as spiritual as they are mental, and until I searched myself and removed the flesh, I would always be fighting. I needed to dig deeper, identify, and deal with my sins and insecurities.

The numbness is felt across our faces, in the ringing of our ears, in that weighted feeling in the center of our chests, and in our swollen eyes. The physical look of our remorse, regret, regression, and wreckage is only a small taste of what we are mentally, emotionally, and spiritually feeling. The root of our sadness stems much deeper than most realize. It's a pain that seems impossible to heal, a shame that we believe will never end, and a constant reminder of our ignorance, iniquity, and repulsive nature. It haunts, taunts, and aims to restrict any breath of optimism and self-worth. We deem our actions and reactions inexcusable and deem ourselves incapable of love. You see, true remorse and shame is not only crippling, but it also has the power to be our most sincere catalyst. Where true conviction meets a contrite heart, true conversion can be created.

- Morgan Richard Olivier

CHAPTER 4
REMORSE

It was beyond heartbreak. It was a *soulbreak* to realize that I was not the person I thought I was. I was a person who could and did hurt others and myself. I suffered in my solitude and felt sincere sorrow, where I felt I belonged, where I could deal with the demon I believed was myself. I needed a place where I could take my consequences and figure it all out one cry, one assessment, one apology, and one day at a time.

I did more than sit in my remorse. I drowned in it. I cried in it. I sulked in it.

> *What are you doing with your life?*
> *What were you thinking?*
> *Who are you?*
> *What is wrong with you?*
> *How could someone like you be so broken, selfish, and destructive like this?*

It seemed as though I had those questions on repeat. I felt like a complete hypocrite. What kind of person writes articles about self-love and positivity yet hates and now sees the negative in everything, especially herself? What kind of person lives to empower others but can be so destructive? How could someone fail to practice what they so commonly preach and truly believe? Who does that?

Those questions came from a place of self-pity and self-loathing. I became paralyzed by it. It consumed my every thought, word, and action. I realized my remorse was not just attached to my current crisis. I had a whole list of reasons to be remorseful. I regretted the times I ignorantly judged others. I felt terrible whenever I remembered the days I could have been better. I replayed failed scenarios of foolish choices and times I knowingly and unknowingly hurt people. I regretted opportunities I didn't take and things I didn't do. It was intense. Maybe the extent to which I took it was beyond seemingly necessary, but the impact and impression it left on me was much needed. It crushed my ego, broke my heart, and seemingly shattered my life as I knew it, but it also fixed my vision and allowed me to see the world and myself through a different lens, a lens that did not come from rose-colored glasses or the comfort of my sheltered life. It created a clear image of who I was and who I didn't want to be. It revealed the part that I played in my life, the lives of others, and this world as a whole. I cried endlessly for the tears and pain I brought to other people. I ripped myself apart daily because, in my heart, I deserved it. It was my selfishness that brought suffering to not only myself but also others. It was my pain that boiled over and burned everything around me.

It seemed like the more I wanted to rid myself of the self-loathing, the more pressure I felt. No amount of shame or guilt could free me from the shackles I felt with every step, and no tangible item could address an intangible unrest that resided within my heart and mind.

However, self-reflection and understanding how I got into this pit did not only make sense of my experiences, but it also provided me with an enlightenment that ensures I will never return to this time in my life. I realized the person who needed the most help, the most change, and the most answers in my life was myself. I got acquainted with acceptance, repentance, and accountability.

REFLECTION

Sometimes, our minds and hearts act as inescapable prisons when we have a conscience. We sit and realize that our words and actions have the power to not only build and destroy us but also positively and negatively affect others. That type of remorse is far more than feeling sorry or apologetic about something we regret. It's identifying, understanding, and ultimately dealing with the responsibility of our wickedness. Our lack of follow through can also add to the weight of remorse. Self-reflection helps us see what we tend to miss. How we treat others and what we say about them matters. Whether we accept this or not, our ignorant opinions and judgments can leave a lasting impression on individuals who are also trying to be better everyday and trying to figure out this thing called life.

Unfortunately, it is out of our hands how others perceive or receive our words or actions. We can't suppress their anger or sadness from our actions, reactions, or words. We can't force them to forgive our foolishness or pacify our problems. As my grandmother used to say: "You have to take your lick to learn your lesson." It would help us all if we understood that we are free to make choices but are not free of the consequences those choices yield.

We've all hurt people knowingly and unknowingly. Oftentimes, what adds to the pain of remorse is our inability to adequately express the scale of remorse we are experiencing. There is a wanting to say or explain but also a knowing that there is a chance it won't be received. It's knowing that "I'm sorry" may be good enough for them but not for us.

Personally, I wish everyone I ever hurt, let down, took for granted, judged, harmed, or manipulated could feel what I truly felt. I wanted them to hear my thoughts, feel the message in the depth of my heart, and understand the sincerity of my sorrow. I wished I could take it all back. I wished they knew my regret. I wished they knew how disappointed I was in myself. No apology could measure up to how I was feeling.

IT COULD BE WORSE

A PSA should be released to the world stating that saying *"It could be worse"* does not take the pain away, and it doesn't make a situation any better. This statement does not silence a condemning voice in anyone's head or make them at peace with a source of chaos. It does not make their anxiety subside or lead them to believe that their crisis is more positive that it appears. Their crisis, whatever it may be or entail, is not up for comparison. "It could be worse" is demeaning to the suffering of an individual.

The more I shared my suffering, the more I heard, "You need to calm down," and "It isn't that serious." I also heard,"It could be worse," and "It's a big deal to you, but your issues aren't that big." Everyone shared the same outlook. They believed I was being too hard on myself. Although that may have been their opinion, that outlook did not ease my pain. It wasn't well with my soul, at all. I tried everything to heal that pain: reading articles, taking medication, reciting prayers, and seeking advice from people who I thought could help me make sense of my problems while giving me rational solutions. I went to doctors, a psychologist, a shaman, an Akashic reader, a psychic, and to Reconciliation. I needed someone to give me direction and a reason as to why I was acting, reacting, and thinking the way that I was. I needed a solution. I needed to feel like everything was going to be okay, even if I couldn't see it at the moment.

I was not being too intense; I was not being too dramatic. I was definitely not overreacting. I was not being too hard on myself or making a mountain out of a molehill. I was suffering a consequence, remorse stricken, more conflicted than ever, and vulnerable. Some days, I was the victim where the world was against me, and other days, I was the aggressor who was just evil. I laid there crying, moaning, hurting, regretting, and searching long enough to realize that the dark cloud I thought I'd come to know was not destruction. It was a chastisement.

REALIZE REALITY

You are human. That weight you are carrying is something you did or failed to do. It is not something that you are. You fell; I get it. Are you just going to stay down forever? Are you just going to throw all of your growth, accomplishments, potential, intelligence, and purpose away because of a fall? Are you going to cease to exist because you messed up, made bad decisions, were rejected, fell short, failed, or that life plan of yours didn't pan out the way you envisioned it? No!

Just as your teachers instructed you whenever you scraped your knees on the playground, just as your parents gave you a dose of tough love whenever you fell off of your bicycle, and just as God is encouraging you in this very season—you can't sit there, cry, and do nothing. You can't be filled with rage and do nothing. You can't be fearful and do nothing. You don't want to feel this way, do those things, or experience those emotions ever again? Then, don't. Get up and make the conscious decision to grow and be better. Keep moving.

Dedicate this time of your life to detach from toxic traits and influences, discover who you truly are, seek deliverance, and develop in the direction that God intended for you to go. It will be far from a cakewalk, but that faith walk will lead you to revelations and blessings you never imagined. I know you may be upset, tired, and even scared, but your journey must continue. You must make the decision to put one foot in front of the other and walk it off. Because no matter how slow, painful, or even silly that walk may seem, you are still moving forward.

Lesson: We can regret and feel all the remorse in the world, but if we don't use that pain to propel us to repent, then we are not only bound to repeat that season of suffering in the future but will also miss out on the beauty of redemption and refinement.

Through God's rebuking, I was able to begin taking the necessary steps to learn who I was because I then knew who I was not.

As time went on, it became clear that I was not a bad person. I was not doomed or destined for failure. I was simply experiencing a very bad time in my life, a season in itself that is normal and natural to others but was just so foreign to me. I realized how I got into this season and why I stayed for so long. I was not a loser. I was lonely, lost, and longing for answers, validation, healing, and more out of my life.

In life, we will all fall, fail, make bad decisions, and find ourselves in seasons where we feel as though the devil has a grip on us. Unfortunately, not everyone escapes from that season finding joy, peace, and strength. Some stay there, but we are not those people.

If there is conviction from remorse, an effort and desire to change, and an awakening to alter ourselves, then that is evidence enough that we are not ruined. Remorse is simply a rough stop on the road to redemption and refinement.

PART II

UNCOVERING AND ADDRESSING UNDERLYING ISSUES

You are allowed to have bad days. You are allowed to struggle to get out of bed. You are allowed to cry, scream, and be angry. You are allowed to not have it all together at all times. However, you are not allowed to give up or throw your life away. These emotions are not new. They have always been tucked, masked, and hidden within you. It's time to focus on your mental and spiritual health, so you can thrive, heal, and deal with all life has for you. God has a way of turning breakdowns into breakthroughs, but first you need to silence the noise.

- Morgan Richard Olivier

CHAPTER 5
ISOLATION

There is a significant difference between being a reclusive slave to depression and taking time to isolate yourself and reflect. Know the difference. Do you want to self-assess, figure things out, or find balance in your life? Take multiple steps back, disconnect from social media, and make a conscious effort to sit in your own solitude. The decision to *simply exist* may come after the best, worst, or most confusing time in your life, but the revelations, realizations, and rest you gain will not only shock you but also open your eyes to some truths about life and the role you're playing in it.

I sat back, listened, and learned more than I ever bargained for. I was able to see how the world actually worked and my deficiency in living and thinking. During that time, I felt and looked like I was breaking, but, really, I was growing in that season. It took silence to grow with God. I was able to hear my thoughts and how I spoke to myself, and, finally, I was able to understand life as it was. I also came to the conclusion that silence is never misquoted, yet it's oftentimes misinterpreted. My silence opened my heart, eyes, and ears to a new meaning of life.

It is isolation that begins the transition in our lives. Isolation can be misunderstood and toxic, but, in this case, it is essential. Much like a caterpillar who retreats from its familiar environment to become a new creature, we must do the same. We have to retreat, analyze, and assess things of the past to make sense of the present, so we can be detoxed, prepared, refined, and ready for our future. Isolation will help us flourish into beautiful versions of ourselves, but before the beauty must come the pain.

It is easy to say everything happens for a reason, but during the lows, everything becomes overwhelming, uncomfortable, and seemingly impossible. A better tomorrow is harder to believe in whenever it seems the whole world is crumbling upon you. Though tomorrow may not come soon enough, isolation can become our refuge. Isolation is a transition phase to a new beginning. It is more than a space of avoidance and fear. It is a place of reflection, acceptance, and protection.

Until you silence the noise, escape expectation, and see yourself and your life for what it is, you never really know what you are working with. You don't know all your weaknesses, and you certainly do not accept why you are weak in those areas. You are unaware of your strengths which leaves you incapable of properly using them. Your season of isolation is more than closing yourself off from distraction, expectation, and the outside world.

It is opening yourself up to see who you are, why you are, and who you were created to be. It is in this space that you learn to be yourself and discover the beauty in the change.

A ROUGH RETREAT

I wanted nothing more than to turn off my phone, hide in a mountain of blankets, and disappear off the face of the Earth. If moving to a deserted island had been an option, I, without a doubt, would have taken it. Instead, I was stuck buried beneath the weight of my worries and the mounds of clothes that I needed to fold at the edge of my bed. I felt like a failure, alone and completely misunderstood. I was a complete mess. Even though people encouraged me to talk to God and claimed He was always with me, I would be lying if I said I believed them. I didn't believe God was near me or that He even cared for my well-being. I was sitting, walking, and living in darkness. I didn't feel His presence. Why would God let me fall so low? Clearly, He didn't care for me or simply didn't want to waste His time on me.

I was angry with God and couldn't understand why He wouldn't deliver me from these emotions and this season all together. If He could do all things, then why was He keeping me in isolation? Why was He not answering my prayers? All I wanted was a sign, anything that would help me escape the Hell I was living. Instead, I felt, saw, and heard nothing. The silence made me question His overall plan for my life and His existence.

Don't get me wrong, with the roller coaster going on within my head and the unrest around me; of course, I wanted silence. However, I received the shock of my life whenever I realized what it meant for silence to be so loud.

It didn't take long to see that whenever you are physically alone and feel mentally, spiritually, and emotionally alone that the silence is almost deafening. It's not because you hear the sound of your lights, air conditioning, and every other tone that is often spoken over. It's because you finally hear the sound of your broken heart, tattered mind, and fragile emotions. The echoes run deep, and the words that reside cannot be ignored. You replay them, analyze them, and seek to understand the words, insults, and cries that are ultimately coming from within your mind and heart.

I was always viewed as the strong friend, role model, and confidant while I was suffering in silence, constantly feeling misunderstood, and secretly seeking mental health therapy for years. While I encouraged everyone around me, I was falling apart and unable to grasp or apply my own encouragement. Realizing and coming to terms with that fact stood out to me.

I began to truly talk to myself. What made that season profound was that I was finally in a position to listen to my actual self. My true motives were exposed, and my fears and frustrations were no longer washed out by the sound of my endeavors or others' opinions. I finally had time to truly reflect on my life and the interest to process it all. Never before did I have such a flood of emotions and memories flow through my head. Memories of traumas I thought I buried long ago, details of dumb decisions that I should have handled differently, and hindsight haunted me to no end. I became acquainted with the side of myself that I didn't want to know and certainly didn't want to exist.

From standing on pedestals and managing perfection to coming face to face with my toxic traits was uncomfortable, shameful, and difficult to accept. It was a time of denial. *Not me.* I'm not manipulative. I'm not controlling. I'm not a people-pleaser. But my self-assessment determined I was not perfect. In fact, it revealed that my image of perfection was just that—an image. I was flawed, and I'd never be perfect because perfection does not exist.

ENLIGHTEN THE DARKNESS

Many times, I felt as if I was walking in complete darkness, and somehow the darkness pierced through my everyday life. It was enlightening, but it was exhausting. Mentally and physically, I could not move forward. Every night, I was in bed by no later than 7p.m., with every blind shut and curtain closed. All I knew was this new darkness. I often spent hours in bed trying to drown out my thoughts with whatever was on television, but even that was not enough. My negative self-talk drove me up the wall. I felt crazy. Other times, the depth of my thoughts comforted me and forced me to confront my inner fears and wildest dreams. I was hidden yet more honest with myself than ever before.

My thoughts helped me dig deeper and understand the importance of discovering who I was and what I was going through. I didn't want to tear myself apart anymore; I wanted to put myself together again. I became introspective and diligent in the pursuit of accepting my actual self and came to terms with my reality. What broke my heart was not simply the isolation, depression, or necessarily everything that led me there. At that point, I felt terrible that I didn't even know who I was. Up until that season of my life, I felt like I had no tough life lessons, no experience, and no ability to pick up the pieces because I simply didn't understand them.

For years, I hid behind my comfort zone and reputation. It became difficult to grow into the woman I was created to be because I was hanging onto the person I always was. I was so concerned about being the good girl that I failed to realize that I needed to evolve into a strong, healthy, and self-aware woman. The pressure to be who I thought others wanted me to be was on me. No one else placed that pressure on me. I did that to myself.

Therefore, the need to be perfect numbed me. I created the perfect life while silently living a depressed, regressed, and suppressed reality.

Though being naïve and protected was something viewed as sweet and wholesome at one time, it had undoubtedly become one of my greatest weaknesses in my adult life. It was not a sign of innocence. It was sheer ignorance. This new realization became part of a crash course to learning the real world. Everything was simply part of the lessons I should have learned long before, so I started from the beginning. I began talking to my psychologist about my earliest memories and, soon thereafter, began healing my inner child.

As a child and young adult, I obsessed over grades and what others thought of me. I based my worth on how much I could get accomplished in a small period of time. As I look back, I clearly see that I didn't *need* to do any of those things. If only I had stepped out of my comfort zone, took time to know myself, and interacted with more people, then maybe I would have had a little more common sense. I could have developed better judgment of others and myself. I would have known then my wants, my fears, my hopes, my weaknesses, and my desires. That was not the case. I was too busy trying to perfect and prove myself. It was isolation and self-reflection that helped me see that my mindset was the stage for my pride and pitfall.

OUR TRUE SELF

We have spent so much time comparing our lives to the world that we have muted our hearts, minds, and intuitions. We live in a time where we have 24-hour, 7-days a week access to an abundance of information at our fingertips, yet so many of us lack knowledge, education, wisdom, and actualization. We crave "being in the know" more than we investigate credibility or the presence of truth. The fact of the matter is that we all hide behind something. We often fail to recognize or accept it until the mask comes off, and life forces us out of our little comfort zones. Whether it's our family roles, social media personas, titles, achievements, or fake smiles, we all find ourselves masked until the person, thing, or idea is no longer available or applicable. When all is left are our truths, it is difficult to recognize. That's when our true selves emerge.

GODLY INTERVENTION

Nothing in life ever happens by chance. There are no coincidences. Everyone and everything in my life was allowed for a reason. Every person, whether I felt they brought out the best or worst in me, was allowed on my path because I needed to learn something from them. God knew which people would cross my path to help me, hurt me, heal me, humble me, and honor me.

I began to see the patterns and placement of things in my life. I realized that many situations, friendships, and even evil was allowed in my life because I was the one attracting them. I had my own toxicity, and I needed God to step in and shift my focus and direction. I began to analyze my motives and those of others. I couldn't continue living the same way. I had to make necessary changes and improve the way I viewed and lived life. I asked myself questions. "Am I doing this because I wholeheartedly believe in the cause or am I seeking validation, respect, and praise?" "Is this person encouraging, validating, and praying for me because they care for me or do they have hidden intentions?" Understanding the motives of others and myself was critical, and I needed all of the wisdom and discernment I could get.

My mindset was my greatest source of pain. Until I fixed that or allowed God to retrain my thinking, I knew nothing else would change. That was the reason why no one's help would 100% heal me. Now, I understand that God was hiding me within my pain, so I could learn how to heal with Him.

Silence and seclusion are your greatest teachers. The ability to stay calm is a superpower, and simply listening and observing will reveal much more than you think. Knowing your weaknesses is not only a testament and response to your humility but also one of the greatest strengths you can have. The devil attacks you at your weakest times and in your weakest areas. If you don't know what and where they are, spiritual warfare is going to certainly drag you until you open your eyes, mind, and spirit to God. With God by your side, you will always have the victory, but you need to understand and acquire the mental and spiritual tools to fight.

God does not isolate you because He wants you to crumble. He isolates you for your own protection and preservation. He is teaching and preparing you. He has a still, small voice. How else could you hear Him unless He put you in a quiet place? In isolation, you have time to seek, hear, and speak to Him.

If you find yourself in this moment of isolation, ask Him, "What are you trying to teach me in this season? What are you trying to protect me from? What in my heart, mind, and life is displeasing to you? What direction do you want me to go in? Reveal to me what you want of me." Don't be shy, and don't be scared. He is waiting to give you the answers, but, first, you must ask.

MORGAN RICHARD OLIVIER

The true journey of self-love, acceptance, and spiritual growth is more complex than sitting on a pew, trying meditations, or reading inspirational quotes. It's accountability while assessing and addressing the person in the mirror. It's understanding that sometimes we are toxic people and that if we don't find, forgive, and fix ourselves, then we will not experience the freedom of actualization or beauty of becoming a new creation. Our life is not about perfection and people-pleasing, and it certainly isn't about the past or being paralyzed by our problems and wrong turns throughout life. It's about applying lessons and pursuing purpose. It is about peace, progression, and being the person you were created to be.

- Morgan Richard Olivier

CHAPTER 6
YOUR MINDSET MATTERS

We can either dwell in the past and negatives we've experienced, or we can grow from them. It doesn't matter if we had a horrible childhood, a failed marriage, or struggled with personal issues our entire lives, we have to make the choices to break away from those times, learn from our struggles, and stand tall. The choice always has been and always will be ours.

When God chastised me, He left me with very important lessons. One that stuck out was the importance of order and the need to be mindful of my actions, motives, and placement. I needed to identify, accept and address myself, my life, and my issues. I needed to search within and access all that pertained to my life, as I found solutions to my problems.

Yes, we all know that we have flaws and quirks, but how often do we take the time to dive in and discover the reasons why? How long does it take for us to identify cycles and reoccurring struggles before we actually do something about them? Instead of harping on the what (what happened, what we did, what we said), the true question we should ask ourselves is *why*. Understanding the "whys" of our thoughts, fears, motives, actions, and reactions is critical in helping us conquer toxic traits and stimulating our growth. Everything in our lives is connected in some form or fashion. It's connecting the dots and making sense of them that uncovers the reason why we are and who we are.

In the midst of my struggles, it seemed like everything I was experiencing, feeling, and doing was leading me up for the final chapter of my life. I experienced all of the pains so deeply: emptiness, confusion, rebellion, remorse, failure, depression, anger, grief, betrayal, and despair. I could have blamed the world, people, and my pain, and, at times, I did. As I sat there and looked at the wreckage of my life, I realized the person who needed the most attention and blame was myself. I needed to do more than simply ask myself "Why me?" I needed to dig deep and discover what seemed like a maze of whys:

Why am I so angry?
Why am I hurting people I love?
Why am I self-medicating?
Why do I struggle to love myself?
Why am I trying to escape the life I always wanted?
Why do I feel the need to please others?

Why do I need the validation of others?

Why am I here?

I realized the answers to my questions couldn't come from anyone else but me. Everything begins and ends with me. Though my pain may not have always been caused only by my poor choices, my healing will always be my responsibility. My life is a reflection of my poor and positive decisions. If I want my life to change for the better, then I must first change for the better. I can't just continue to compartmentalize pain and think its impact and effects will just disappear. I can't just think or behave badly and believe that, in time, it will be sorted out. It was time to focus on my mental health and what truly mattered in my life.

MENTAL HEALTH

The choice to seek mental health counseling saved my life, and the daily choice to seek spiritual counseling continues to save my soul. Before, what most would consider my Quarter-life Crisis or mental breakdown, I made it a point to attend counseling. For over two years, I went to discuss my irrational fears, low self-esteem, anxiety, and depression. Most of all, I discussed how I could better deal with the people around me, how to deal with family, adapt to stress in marriage, and how to better focus my energy on myself. I absolutely loved my doctor and the results acquired. I could tell I had grown and so could others. In turn, the local paper interviewed me on the importance of mental health counseling. My answer was simple. I shared that I had only begun living in the months following therapy. I believed it then and still believe it now. Therapy was a safe space where I could exhale without bias or judgment. I was able to talk about anything and everything, which helped me heal and live fully.

I took a break from my sessions until I couldn't ignore the spiral. I knew I needed help, and the only way to get through whatever I was going through was to figure it out within myself.

There were intense sessions where the subject matter not only surprised my doctor but also shocked me. The level, depth, and sacredness of what I shared drastically changed. I felt that I just had to get everything out whether it was past, present, or fear of the future. Once I saw myself as the person who people needed to deal with, my direction and demeanor changed. I was the person who was undoubtedly hurting people and hurting myself. I was the type of person I didn't want to be or felt I could never become.

Something in me was bad, and I was not going to stop searching until I removed and detoxed from whatever it was. You see, as long as I viewed my issues as a response to someone or something else, I was still living in my ego. I needed to address my pain and the problems that so heavily bothered me. I was at war with myself, lying, and putting Band-Aids on mental bullet wounds. I was only positioning myself to create wars with everyone else. Everything was beginning to boil over. My anger, strife, resentment, sadness, insecurity, and madness were not new to me. They were buried within me.

Yeah, I could blame anyone and anything, but here I am — not my husband, not my friends, not my enemies or anyone else for that matter. Here I am in this psychologist's office — teary eyed, looking like a deer in headlights, bewildered and broken because I can't seem to make sense of the persistent pain, poor decisions, severe depression, and overwhelming darkness in my outwardly perfect life. I can't blame the world for that. There's obviously something wrong within me for this crisis to be going on around me. All those solo car rides and long showers filled with crying caught up with me. All those days I sat back and judged the life choices and rationale of others came back to bite me. The traumas I always tried to bury came out from their graves. The instances where I could have reached out to someone but chose to sit back and play the strong role created a weakness and blind spot in me that only I could correct.

ACCOUNTABILITY

Of all the issues I've had or believed I had in my life, my mouth and my mindset made everything worse. I had to learn to take responsibility for my actions and understand that there is a difference between empathetic, irrational, emotional, and ignorant responses.

We have to stop pointing the finger at everyone and everything and take a long, deep look within ourselves. Blaming others will not take our negative experiences away. Living a lie will not take away the underlying truth. Compartmentalizing all of our most painful traumas will not make our mental and physical scars go away. There comes a time that we must realize that we can be those toxic people holding us back.

We get hit with seasons of uncertainty, lack of understanding, and the need to find our place. We begin to overanalyze our existence. Much worse, it begins to feel like the beginning of the end or a road filled with never ending bumps. At first, accountability feels somewhat like an attack. Whether it's a childhood trauma, present day crisis, or a situation that brought suffering into our lives, unwrapping and dissecting our hard times and patterns of behavior can be extremely difficult. It's like opening an old wound. It's removing what appeared to be a protective layer and dowsing it in alcohol. It's for our overall good, but it hurts like Hell to address.

MIRROR, MIRROR

You can blame your childhood, parents, spouse, friends, family, enemies, insecurities, disabilities, finances, and everyone under the sun, but until you direct your attention to the person in the mirror, you will continue to suffer. You will continue to be stuck. You will continue to waste your time and energy. Direct your attention to your ego. Blame your stagnation on your inability to adapt to change. Understand that it's your unwillingness to identify and dissect your inner demons that keeps you from clarity and alignment.

Before pointing fingers at others, make a point to assess yourself. As long as you're blaming, you aren't growing. As long as you're living in the past, you aren't dealing with the present or preparing for the future. Rid yourself of the notion that someone else will waltz into your life and save the day. You are responsible for the happiness and wholeness of your life. The world can give you many things, but it can't give you wisdom, peace, or love. That is up to you.

THE BALL IS IN YOUR COURT

No matter how old, esteemed, or stable we may appear, we are all hungry for something, and we all know a starving person will accept anything to fill the void in his or her belly. Some crave power, a rush or wealth, while others crave acceptance, a sense of freedom, or some form of peace. No matter what the craving is, it is a driving force in our lives. If not properly directed, it can drive us to have very dark days. An issue of the heart and the aspiration of artificially filling voids has the power and capability to become a block in our pursuit of happiness, purpose, relationships, and future.

After walking in circles, wandering the world for clarity, and falling on our faces, we stop waiting around and accept that our healing will never come from our friends, family, tangible things, medication, or some catchy quote. It has to come from within. There is always a root to our fruit. Many of us seek validation because we fear rejection. We overcompensate on social media because we aren't where we want to be in reality. We are critical of others because the flaws we see in them are also buried within ourselves. Projection is common, but it will not help us in the slightest bit. We must look within ourselves, both thoroughly and honestly, if we want to progress. After all, it's the mind that tells us how and when to move.

It is said that we can't control *what* we see in the world, but we can control how we see it. Those mountains may always be there, and we may never like to be around those people. We may still have mental and emotional struggles, but the burdens seem lighter whenever we can better face and understand ourselves. When we can finally look in the mirror and not see just brokenness but a resilient human being, we realize that the solitude, darkness, and storms we've been so scared of weren't here to destroy us. They were here to enlighten us, condition us, prune us, and turn our fear into faith.

- Morgan Richard Olivier

CHAPTER 7
THE JOURNEY INWARD

The most uncomfortable and life-changing roads we will encompass are those concerned with the journey inward. It is the true assessment of "self." Whether we embark on the mission after a crisis, experimental phase, or on the cusp of elevation, one truth can't be denied. Once we dig deep, it's clear that we were blindly shallow before. It is an apparent wake-up call that there is so much more to us than meets the eye and so much to detox, discover, and develop.

Think of our mindsets, influences, and beliefs as a compass. Whether we realize it or not, we tend to go in the direction they take us. However, routines and comfort zones tend to derail us from aligning our lives to where we actually want them to go. What if the routes we know and love leave us with no opportunity to elevate? What if the direction we are going will lead to nothing but detours, dead ends, and destruction? What if all the energy, sweat, and tears we are putting into our current life journeys are actually leading us in circles? Self-assessment is essential to redirecting our journey. Our lives won't change until we do.

The renewing of our minds is a powerful and impactful process—a series of enlightenments that allows us to not only view ourselves through another lens but also have the unbiased ability to look in the past and dissect the errors of our ways. We discover that taking steps back from the routines, practices or being the people we're *accustomed or expected to be* actually increases our levels of self-actualization. To analyze, understand, and align ourselves—we have to isolate, investigate, and accept all that we truly are. Whether we take a psychological, spiritual, or combination of both approaches to self-assessing—the level of discomfort, humility, and even sensitivity will inevitably increase. We discover that we aren't perfect people, and we will never be. It is not because we messed up in the past or because we are struggling today. It's also not because we aren't beautiful enough or need to improve in some way. It's because the definition of perfection is not only relative, but also unattainable. We begin to see who we are, and that isn't always what we expected or know.

As prim, proper, and consistently happy as we may have always appeared, we have to be honest with ourselves. Not all that glitters is gold. We have blind spots, weaknesses, and toxic traits that we need to address and abort. Instead of covering up and compartmentalizing the pain, we must acknowledge our shortcomings. We have undoubtedly fallen short, silently struggled, let ourselves down, experienced trauma, got into messy situations, and simply have issues we must correct. As shocking and even disheartening as that may be for most of us to accept, it's the sincere acknowledgment that aligns us with our actualization. We identify and, for the first time understand, just how imperfect we are and the things we need to work on. We do so not in a condemning way but in a way that convicts and encourages us to do and be better. Moreover, we begin to learn and unlearn things about ourselves, the world around us, and the functionality of our mindset and motivations. We see just how much our perspective, experience, and willingness to evolve affects us mentally, spiritually, and emotionally.

Realignment and change can feel like complete and utter chaos, but change from complacency is a necessity. We realize that all things are connected and that—until we understand, express, feel, and close the doors of the past—we will never be able to fully live in the present or prepare ourselves for the future. Therefore, we face the facts of our lives. Hindsight may haunt us, and reopening and repenting from wounds and strongholds may heal us. Ultimately, though, the idea of new adventures excites us. What's most important is that it alters our mindsets. We accept the truth that once we change our mindset, we also change our lives, hearts, and directions. Our focus becomes the people underneath it all and the potential and purpose that must be realized. We discover that all that time we felt lost and ill-equipped, everything we needed was already within us. Behind all our pain was power, and, aside from our flaws, always stood our talents and passions without blemish. Even at our most vulnerable, we embodied strength.

As we evolve to know who we are and make peace with our authenticity, we stop trying to convince others of who we are and slowly put people-pleasing to rest. We see ourselves as a work in progress that must cut dead weight to reach higher heights. Though we may not be exactly where we want to be, we are grateful to know we aren't where we once were. We are humbled, empowered, refined, and ready for what lies ahead. When we begin to accept who we are, we let go of the pressure to seek the approval and praise of others.

Facing my faults, flaws, and failures was difficult but necessary. I needed to accept that life was not a fairytale and focus on what mattered. I knew nothing would ever be the same, and it shouldn't be. If I had not reached this unbearable point, I would still be stuck in a maze, repeating the same cycles, and bound to stagnation, searching, suffering, and starving for discernment like I once was. There was no going back to the previous version of myself. I needed to accept who I had been to ascend to where I was supposed to go.

Discovering, developing, and discussing the positive points of life and self is easy, but acknowledging and accepting the negative and nonsensical is difficult. It's an extremely uncomfortable and humbling process. However, we can't fix our flaws until we face the facts of what they are.

I'm not without flaws. I'm not perfect. I'm not an angel. I'm not some invincible person who's only capable of excellence and has never fallen on her face. I've fallen short many times. I've hurt and have been hurt. I've been a hypocrite, doubter, liar, cheater, loser, runner, backstabber, miser, coward, manipulator, and fool. I've acted and reacted out of fear, desperation, impulse, resentment, frustration and have done irresponsible, ignorant, and irrational things. I've judged, spoke, and discredited without understanding. From a place of remorse and acceptance, coming to terms with those negative facts hurt. I dwelled on them to the point that all I saw were my flaws, failures, and foolishness.

But the journey within is not one sided. It embraces both the good and the bad. Yes, I may have done or said bad things, but I've also been a good person. I have given with no intent of ever being repaid, gone out of my way to do the right thing, and treated people with respect. I have always looked for the good in people, even if they couldn't see it for themselves, and loved unconditionally. I have been genuinely compassionate, friendly, considerate, patient, understanding, intelligent, comforting, kind and loving. There is more than one side to me, and I can't just ignore one while I elaborate the other.

Like everyone else, I'm a flawed human who is just trying to get her life, soul, and mind together. For a long time, I was oblivious to that fact. I was so busy trying to minimize my flaws that my motives were creating more. If I wanted my life right then, I needed to get my mind, motives, and spirit right. I needed to focus on what mattered and shut everything else out.

It's not like I woke up one morning and completely stopped caring about the opinions of others. It's that I gradually became concerned and aware of my own. I discovered the importance of being well with myself. I began to realize just how much of my life I had given away to the pursuit of perfection and fear of rejection. That certainly was no way of living, so I promised myself I would never view my worth through the lens of insecurity again. It was time to dive in, discover, and develop who I truly was. It was freeing and healing to tap into my hidden talents and passions, while putting that once wasted energy into fiercely fighting for and protecting my purpose.

For a long time, I struggled to fully accept the person in the mirror. I wanted to change everything about her. As I reflected, I became more curious of who that person in the mirror actually was. I wanted to get to know her, love her, forgive her, embrace her, and always remind her that she always has been and always will be good enough. She wasn't perfect, but her heart was pure and her mind, beautiful. That in itself was captivating to me.

I decided to place myself in an environment that fed my intellect but starved my ego. I reverted to things that I loved as a child: art, educational programs, and simply sitting on the backyard swing listening to the wind blow. I began to fall in love with myself and who I was becoming. I was perfectly imperfect and that was more than okay. The feeling was foreign, but it felt so natural and right. I saw myself in a new light. It was a long time coming, but if I wanted to remain on that course, I had to protect my mind, peace, and purpose and understand that no transformation will ever come easy. My attempts and realignment were prone to attacks, and I was ready to protect and defend.

I spent quality time with myself and found peace in the process. I began writing down my thoughts and benchmarking. I identified patterns, became aware of my triggers, and noticed a change in the way I perceived life and myself. There was so much more to me than I ever realized—natural talents that were hidden beneath my fear of failure, strengths that surprised me, and a confidence that was slowly coming to the forefront. I was healing but also slowly honing in on who I was. My mind needed healing and attention more than I realized. Until I got my mind right, I couldn't get my soul right.

Without the renewing of our minds, all is lost. For example, our finances cannot flourish if we are too impulsive to save or invest. Our relationships will suffer if we can't communicate or find a way to sort through even the most basic issues. We will not be able to accomplish our goals or grow in any capacity until we rid ourselves of childish thinking, negative self-talk, or irrational fear. We need wisdom, self-control, empathy, and our thoughts rooted in truth if we want anything in our lives to blossom.

The mind is powerful yet fragile. Feed it truth and forgiveness, and transform your thinking if you seek to transform your life. The world will tell you many things and tempt you to follow its paths, but it will not show you how to get to God, how to reach your destination, or who you truly are.

MORGAN RICHARD OLIVIER

I long for a place that I always belonged. Where peace is created and openly given. A place where the walls serve as a shelter from the bad but manifests all that is good, where I can come as I am but leave better than I was before.

- Morgan Richard Olivier

CHAPTER 8
A DWELLING PLACE

Just when I thought I could catch a break, the waves of depression always put me under. There was always another argument, another setback, another breakdown, another issue, another sickness, and another problem. It went on for months. The worst wave was when my grandmother got sick to the point that she was not going to get better. We always shared a bond that was beyond words and understanding. For the last decade, she battled and lost her memory to Alzheimer's Disease. Now, she was about to lose her life. I felt helpless because I knew there was nothing I could do. I spent so much of the last months of my life crying, falling apart, withdrawing from everyone and everything, and working on myself that I completely forgot about her. I didn't visit her like I should have because I was so wrapped up in myself and my own problems. Now, here we are running out of time.

For the final weeks of her life, I never left her side. I held her hand every chance I could get, sang our old songs, and just enjoyed her presence as long as I could. I apologized for my absence and poured out my heart. I wanted her to know just how much I loved, appreciated, and needed her not only in this part of life but also in the next.

My grandmother's passing felt like my breaking point. The sadness of confusion was one thing, and the pain of regret and depression was another. Altogether, the cut associated with death was something I just couldn't handle. It was a devastating feeling of emptiness. I just couldn't wrap my mind around the idea that she was gone.

At the funeral home, it brightened my spirits to see family and friends come together. As we all gathered, I began chatting with my aunt. She mentioned that she missed reading my articles since I had not posted any in months. I was shocked. I didn't even know she read them. I didn't think she would notice my absence.

I tried to give her a good "fluffed" response, a response that wouldn't tip off any concerns or make her think I was a "hot mess." She stopped me mid-sentence and said, "You're going through depression." I tried to deny it, but she said it was written all over my face, in my energy, and the way I talked. She said she knew because she had once been there before. She went as far as describing how my house likely looked and the emotions I was feeling. She was spot on. She began to share her experience with depression and consoled me. She mentioned that spiritual warfare was hard and that the enemy wanted her life, but she overcame. At the moment, I wanted to deny her discovery, and I also felt extremely confused. I didn't even know what spiritual warfare was. She ended by praying with me and for me, and she invited me to church that Saturday. She claimed it was life-changing. At that point, I figured "Why not?" I was already paying for doctors, trying to pray, and—honestly—I just needed a good fix. If this church was my only hope, then I was open to it.

When Saturday night service came, it seemed like everything was going wrong. I couldn't find my keys, and my car was out of gas. The traffic was terrible, and I took the wrong turn. Everything seemed chaotic, but thanks to my GPS, I made it.

It was a small building, but the parking lot was full. I parked in front of the Glory Victory Church sign; I could hear the music before I even opened my door. As I walked into the church, the pastor greeted me and said, "I've been waiting for you" and walked me to the seat that I still occupy today. Even though everything about this place was new, I was overwhelmed with a sense of peace and comfort. It was like everything leading up to this day had been waiting for me. It was an amazing feeling. I literally wept the entire service. It was intense yet liberating. I felt free and light. I knew I was in the right place at the right time. I knew I would be coming back, and I was exactly where I was supposed to be. For the first few months, I cried every service. Whether it was silent tears or open sobs, it was therapeutic. My tears were releasing all of my pain. Even though my struggles were very much real and still present, something deep inside me was changing. As each service passed, the person who walked out felt completely different than the person who walked in.

As I became more invested and involved with the Church, my pastor became my confidant, wise counsel, and spiritual advisor. Her gift of vision, compassion, and wisdom not only comforted me but also convicted me to grow closer to God and seek His wisdom. Only He could order my steps, and only I could put in the work to follow them. As our relationship grew, we spoke deeply about everything I was going through, and she helped me heal. Eventually, I substituted my psychologist with prayer and fasting. Though that may not be an option for all people, depending on their diagnoses and situations, it was the right time and season for me. It was time to truly live again. Now, this time is with God.

Remember when I was in the pit of my pain? I couldn't do anything. As a person who loved to write, sing, and dance, I didn't have the strength, will, or desire to do a single thing. What is there to sing and dance about when you don't even want to exist anymore? What is there to write about when you feel like your hope is gone? I believed that I couldn't write about life when I obviously was not living it well. Who would want advice from a failure? I was throwing my voice, my gift, and my power away because it felt like I had been in my pit for too long. I made my time of sorrow a shackle, but that monologue changed whenever I put God into everything.

I felt like I was beginning to recharge whenever I protected my energy and spirit. With time, I started writing again. I didn't originally start writing with the intent to share. It was a way to release my thoughts and get my mind moving again. I wrote about my life, my lessons, and what it was like to truly feel lost in this world. Although the subject matter was not bright and bubbly like my old articles used to be, those pieces felt and impacted me more significantly because they were raw and messy. I was able to dive into the messages that the messes of life left me. I felt empowered. What felt like the worst experiences of my life were teaching me to better empathize with others and express myself. I was on a new and improved path, and there was no turning back. I found what I had been missing. I could stop searching because I didn't feel empty anymore. I truly found God, my place, and my desire to thrive.

CHURCH GUILT

I absolutely loved this new church. I loved the peace I was gaining, the growth I was experiencing, and the relationships that were blossoming. Most of all, I loved feeling so close to God. I felt like I belonged. Every service seemed like it spoke directly to me, and I was learning so much about the Bible, God, and myself. However, I grew doubtful. In the back of my mind, I wondered if

I was messing up. I felt guilty for my joy, peace, and growth. How could someone experience God and guilt simultaneously? Who does that? In time, I realized that many people experience those same feelings.

Up until that point in my life, all I knew was Catholicism. I attended private Catholic schools, pre-k through 12th grade. I received all of my sacraments from Baptism to Marriage. Not to mention, I was a Godmother—a person who swore to help rear a child in the Catholic faith. I was supposed to be Catholic forever, but here I am going to another church. This new church was so enjoyable that I questioned if it was right. It felt like I was disrespecting or turning my back on the Catholic foundation instilled in me. I began to question my actions. "Does this service count? Is this a test from God? Am I attending the right church?"

Because I had this new bold love and fear of upsetting God, I solved my problem in the most practical way I found fit. I started doubling up services. I would go to Glory Victory on Saturday nights and then go to the Catholic Mass on Sundays. Don't get me wrong. The added services really did make a positive difference, but, over time, I had to check my motives and ask myself why I was feeling and responding to this church dilemma the way I was.

Was I wrong by worshipping at another church, or did it just feel wrong because it was something new? What will my family think? Will they believe I'm making a bad decision or that

I'm turning away from everything I had been taught in the Catholic Church? What does this mean for the future of my faith? Most importantly, what does this mean for the faith of my future children? Will they not be baptized? Can I still go to Catholic functions? What does this all mean for me?

It wasn't so much the title that concerned me. It was the relationship. Where was I going to grow more spiritually? Where did He want me to be?" I had to silence my mind and stop trying to figure everything out. I needed to have faith and know that if God wanted me somewhere, He'd make it known. If He wanted me to move, He'd somehow make that known, as well. This wasn't a time or decision to base on uncertainty, opinions, or even my feelings. I was serious about the course of my faith, my growth, and my relationship with God, so I did what I had been taught. I gathered my concerns and cares and took it up with God. I prayed about it, promised to fully obey and surrender to whatever direction, and put it in His hands. After much time and honest praying, I found peace in knowing that my new church was my place, and I was exactly where I needed to be. I later took the plunge and got baptized. With the support of my husband, family, and friends there—I took a critical step in my journey and have not looked back since.

My church home decision was not based on a trend, fickle feelings, or overall approval. It was true alignment and one of the most important, life-altering stepping stones on my journey. In many ways, committing to my church, getting baptized, and understanding my role was my first real act of obedience. I wouldn't take back that decision for the world.

Spiritual structure and support is important. It's more than just the church we walk into or the title that we cling to. It's about building a relationship with God and doing so in an environment that supports and encourages that growth. Anyone can claim to be a Christian, sit in a pew, and look the part, but God is not looking for actors. He is looking at our hearts and wants us to do much more than associate with a church. He wants us to be the church.

PART III

FINDING RELEASE AND REVELATIONS

When I was down and at my worst, Jesus didn't turn away from me, talk about me, or deem me unworthy. He didn't look down on me or make me feel like there was no coming back. He didn't remind me of my shortcomings or make me feel less than. He didn't fabricate my foolishness or exaggerate my iniquities. He had mercy on me. He showed compassion whenever all I could see was chaos and confusion. He tended to my wounds, listened to my cries, and was attentive to every one of my concerns. As much as I couldn't physically see Him or touch Him, I—for the first time in my life—undeniably felt Him with me. I felt His peace whenever I would just open up to Him and do so completely. He was there for me whenever I couldn't even be there for myself.

- Morgan Richard Olivier

CHAPTER 9
THE LOVE OF GOD

Even when I didn't know how to put into words how I felt, God made sense of it all. He understood me and led the way to my healing. While working on myself, I was able to hear Him and obey His commands. God wanted the best for me, and I was learning to trust Him. It was critical that I not only built my trust and relationship with God but also truly loved Him and learned to love and emulate what pleases Him. I allowed myself to become an instrument of love. I needed to show love to others without ego or exception and work on myself from the inside out. That is where accountability and an honest assessment of myself met my desire to completely transform—no matter the cost or what the world would perceive as a loss. All of the revelations of myself and of my surroundings were needed to detox and develop the new creature I was becoming.

I began to detox my mind, my friends, my music, my wardrobe, and my life. I gave away clothes that may not have been inappropriate to the world but were not in line with the woman I was working to become. I stopped associating and reaching out to people, places, and things that were not able to stimulate, accept, or want the growth that I desperately desired. I also removed songs from my playlist that negatively affected my spirit and replaced them with music that improved my mood and my praise. As hard as I thought letting go of my former life was at times, it was also refreshing to me. It was a slow removal of dead weight, worry, and worldly expectations. I was taking on a new identity in Christ.

As this new journey unfolded, I began to learn more about my family history and the importance of understanding spiritual warfare. I always thought generational curses were fictional, but I learned that strongholds were in fact very real. My past battles had built me up for tough moments in spiritual warfare. I felt like each step forward was taking me further away from the shackles and closer to freedom. I was hooked on God and did not want to stop learning and growing. I found purpose in life again. I was singing, leaving the house, finding joy throughout the day, and actually laughing again.

I can remember praying to God for discernment, direction, and to make my desires in line with His. I was so in love with the mental, spiritual, and emotional growth I was experiencing. The transformation made me not only want to talk to God more but also become more in line with Him. I wanted further revelation to go along with my revival and redirection. I wanted every aspect of my heart, mind, and life to be refined. If there was someone or something standing in the way of my refinement, I wanted it to be revealed to me and within me. Sounds great doesn't it? Was the experience great? Well— that's to be greatly debated.

With my new life came new vision and the need to address more. The spiritual blindness was slipping away, but it left me with the image of a broken world and many pieces of my life that needed to either be repaired, protected, or discarded all together. I began to see my own toxicity and the venom I allowed into my life in the form of friends, family, and influences. I saw my motives, fears, and ignorance and the roles that they played in my actions, reactions, and plans.

Unfortunately, my new life was not always accepted or understood by all of my friends and family. While I had friends who loved transformation, I had other people who called me obsessed and even mocked my conversion. People who were not "saved" were always somehow the ones scrutinizing the validity of my salvation. Did it hurt my feelings and frustrate me at times? Yes, of course! At times, it really angered and upset me, especially whenever it was people who had no issue seeing me struggle, yet they tried to discredit or derail the joy I found from transforming my life. However, everyone is entitled to his or her own opinion, and it doesn't mean it has to hinder my growth. I was on a mission to become a better version of myself. Nothing and no one was going to stop me.

The more I felt under spiritual attack or misunderstood, the more I loved and looked for words, numbers, and acts of confirmation. With everything I was feeling, I needed them to help me stay the course and to help me not lose sight of my destination especially whenever the distractions seemed to never end. I commonly found myself in what I thought were coincidental situations where a person would give me a message that related to a verse I read or a message from God that I meditated on. In reality they weren't coincidences at all. They were all signs that I was on the right track. God made a way for me, sent confirmations, and reminded me to keep going. It's not because He owed it to me or that I was entitled. I received His messages because I worked to keep the obedience, conversation, and relationship open.

TALK TO HIM

Tell Him what you're feeling and what you're going through, and ask for His help. It seems unnecessary to discuss something like that to a God who is supposed to know your every action, thought, and word, but He wants it. You need to seek Him in order to truly grow.

It took what I viewed as a lot of unanswered prayers to understand God's answers. I prayed more in that season of crisis and confusion than I ever had in my entire life, and still I felt there was nothing. I was still stuck, and I didn't hear or see a difference. I just wanted God to tell me, straight up, what to do. I honestly believed that if I talked to God, He would quickly and surely answer. Therefore, I didn't want a sign, some whisper in the wind, or short-lived encouragement. I wanted Him to clearly, boldly, and miraculously make this life-altering statement that I couldn't ignore. I wanted an answer, command, or idea that not only gave me direction but also brought me instant peace. I—for some reason—felt I deserved something, as if me returning to Him made me entitled to that information.

As time passed and my troubles didn't, I grew impatient. I felt ignored, upset, and unsure of what I could be doing so wrong to where God wouldn't just tell me what to do to make my life right. I was tired of suffering, tired of feeling confused, and beyond tired of feeling like I was reliving cycles. I was growing and joyful one day and then miserable and drained the next. I felt like I was in the midst of the most drawn out storm I had ever experienced.

"What do you expect from me? Do you even hear me? Do you hate me? How am I supposed to look to you for strength, guidance, and direction if you don't even want to acknowledge me? Why do you have selective responses?" That's what I honestly asked God. Through time and prayer, I was able to understand that no answer was His answer. As crazy as it sounds, He wanted me to cry to Him, and He wanted me to struggle to fix the pieces of my life. He wanted me to see my life for what it was. More than anything, He wanted me to realize and truly digest what my life was *without* Him. He wanted me to understand that nothing was in order, in balance, or in agreement because I failed to put Him first in it. He wasn't going to fix a thing until I got my mind right and fixed my spiritual vision enough to understand that what He was trying to fix was me. Everything around me was undoubtedly an issue, but what was of His concern was what was going on within me: my poor mindset and my relationship with Him that needed more work.

For any relationship to work, it takes communication. God works just the same. If I wanted Him to talk and answer me, then our relationship should not be one-sided. I shouldn't just call Him whenever I need something. I should be constant and not conditional. Our bond should be real. It took longer than it probably should have for me to accept that fact, but I learned that if I wanted my health, marriage, career, relationships, and mind to be in order, then I had to have him in the lead. I had to give up my control and follow Him.

Now, God is my go-to. Before I make decisions, I consult Him. After I succeed at any endeavor, I truly thank and acknowledge Him. If I feel lost or unsure of how to feel or react to something, I pause and pray on it. Whenever I feel confused, I seek God's understanding and pray for clarity that only He can give me. Whatever I want for my life, or think I want for my life at the time, I run it by Him and see if it aligns with His plans. If it will bring me peace, prosperity, or progression—I ask that He bless it. If it will bring problems, pain, and push me out of alignment—then I simply ask that He block it. That's it. That way, no matter what happens, I have peace in knowing that it's a part of His greater plan and is the best course of action for my life. Even if it may not have been my original choice, I know His choice always makes a better way for me.

WEEPING MAY ENDURE

One morning, I woke up drained, depressed, and feeling completely done with everything. I got in my car, and, as soon as I got out of the driveway felt safe in my own solitude, the tears just started flowing. It had become a routine at that point, bawling the entire 15-minute drive to work. I didn't care who passed me on the highway and saw or if I looked like a complete basket case breaking down at the stop light. Some mornings, I simply couldn't control it, and that morning was definitely one of them. It was then that I felt engulfed in my own pity and pain and internally asked God, "Why are you doing this to me? Why is misery following me like a dark cloud? Haven't I suffered enough?

Haven't I lost enough weight? Haven't I prayed enough? Haven't I cried enough? Can't you see that I'm barely hanging on? Why would you want me to be like this?" Not even 10 seconds after my pity party, my phone vibrated. It was a text from my best friend. Though the lock screen prevented me from reading the entire text message at glance, I was able to look over and see the first line of her message that read "Weeping may endure for a night, but joy comes in the morning." It stopped me in my tracks. That can't be God responding to me through her can it? For a minute, there were no tears and no wallowing. I just sat there moved by what had just happened.

Unfortunately, as fast as the peace came from reading that verse, it quickly left. Weeping may endure *for a night?* I wish! This weeping has been going on for far more than a night. Obviously, this verse either doesn't apply to me, or that's just God's way of hitting me with some poetry. As God would have it and time would pass, He would show me exactly what He meant. The verse did not manifest to an end of my problems, but it planted a seed that I would be able to revert to once I progressed and learned more on my journey.

Our time is not equivalent to God's time. We know this whenever we think about The Story of Creation and compare it to science. God's single day could be millions of years, for all we know. This is why we need to not lean on our own understanding. I know now that God was using my friend to not only give me that message but also made it to where I would never forget that day and the lessons that would tie into that verse. He made it stand out enough that I can vividly remember imagery, words, and emotions from that morning. I learned that the verse, though beautiful, is not literal. Unless we're dealing with a 24-hour laundromat, the stains and pains of our lives are seldom worked out overnight. However, it is the time that allows us to grow.

We sit there picking ourselves apart, wondering why we haven't experienced "that season" yet. We're getting messages of confirmation that we will win, God's going to turn it around, and our pain will turn into our power, yet we feel like all we're doing is consecutively taking punches and can't even enjoy a moment because we're waiting for the next issue. Have we not put in the work? Have we not given our lives to Christ and become the most genuine and growth-minded people we know? Does He not see? He must not know because, if He did, we wouldn't still feel this way: stagnant and suffering. The enemies we wish would just disappear wouldn't constantly attack us. We wouldn't still be so bogged down.

It's important that we remember that time is not an issue with God. In time, God can work things together for our good. However, time is oftentimes a tool manipulated, fabricated, and used by the enemy. The enemy wants us to be entangled in what seems to be a never-ending cycle, so that we get tired and give up. He wants us to begin believing the lie that we had more happiness, peace, and calm before God. The enemy makes low points feel like life sentences when—in actuality—God can turn anyone, any situation, and anything around in His time. The key is to remember that God's time is not ours.

Had God moved at the times and in the ways that I wanted Him to, I wouldn't be the person that I am today. I needed to wait, I needed to learn, and—quite frankly—I needed to suffer. He used the pressure and pain because He was preparing me and pruning me for something greater. Great things take time.

Why are you going through this? Why is this taking so long? The answer is because there is something much bigger at play. There are lessons that need to be learned for your wisdom, faith, and strength to take shape. With your new lessons, you'll be able to walk out of your generational curses, irrational fears, and toxic ways and into your new life. You have to go through the fire to come out refined. All things work together and by faith; this will work too (Romans 8:28 NIV).

FOCUS ON GOD

Far too often, we allow our pity parties and disappointments to blind us from seeing the ultimate purpose of life's pains. We struggle to discern the difference between losses versus the removal of things that are hindering our lives. Is it uncomfortable? Definitely. No matter how it feels, what others think, or if it doesn't fit into our plan, we have to remember that God sees far beyond what we can see and will destroy a mindset, friendship, relationship, or plan before it destroys us. It may be confusing, difficult, and seemingly impossible to accept, but we have to give it to Him. How else will we make room for our blessings? Take a deep breath and remember that hard times don't last forever. We will come out of this refined by fire and ready for all God has promised.

This time of your life may be the hardest, most confusing, and loneliest, but in due time— you will see God never left your side. He's fighting battles you aren't even aware of and carrying you through the days that seem so hard to manage. He's there with you. He's there for you. He's there in you. He said it Himself that He won't leave you or forsake you (Hebrews 13:5). This dark and painful season is the turning point of your life. It's okay to not be okay. Everyone encounters those moments, but it's important to keep moving forward and overcome difficult situations. It is in those moments of life that everything and everyone tells you to give up, but that still small voice tells you to keep going. When God is in our midst, we should not fear. No weapon formed against us shall prosper (Isaiah 54:17).

Our praise and determination in times of pain and doubt will push us forward. God will provide us with strength, and He will delight in our perseverance. The plans that God has for us are greater than we can imagine, so we can't stay down. We must get up, fight hard, and remember that God is with us. The fire in our hearts and in our testimonies will help others run to refinement and alignment with God. Because of our endurance and obedience, others will be able to walk in victory. It takes all of our tears and fears to make us a powerful force against darkness. Our light will be able to shine for others who are lost and also lead our way into peace and growth.

Pain helps us move toward healing while discovering our true selves. Pain is not our destination; it is our stepping stone to everything we have been called to do. Never forget that God can turn our worst into our best. Whatever we have been through will shape us into who God wants us to be. With our experience, we can change the trajectory of our lives and those around us. In realizing that, begin to see that all of its twists and turns are not merely coincidental. Every trial and triumph serve as stepping stones toward repentance, redemption, and refinement so that we too can be redirected, restored, and revel in all that God has for us.

Therefore, cry if you must, and remember that God sees every drop. Keep pushing, keep praying, and keep the faith. Hard times won't last forever, but the lessons will.

MORGAN RICHARD OLIVIER

MORGAN RICHARD OLIVIER

You can't love people to your fullest capacity and harbor a hate of yourself. You can't wholeheartedly walk into your new season if you are carrying the baggage of the old. However, you can choose to let go. Let go of unforgiveness, past pains, and setbacks so that you can open your arms to freedom, a fresh start, and a major comeback. Let go of the unrealistic expectations for yourself and celebrate the work in progress and the powerful person you are. Let go of the bitterness towards others and negative experiences so that you can live, feel, and be better. Let go, so you can learn and latch on to greater. Love covers, and forgiveness frees. It's time to move onward and upward into acceptance and actualization without the weight of anger and fear.

- Morgan Richard Olivier

CHAPTER 10
LET IT GO

Time heals all. Does that sound familiar? We tell that to people in the midst of their depression, people who have lost loved ones and those who can't seem to find their ways out of the ruts of life. It's a light and comforting phrase that seems convincing, but—at its core—is very misleading. For some reason, we believe time itself will hide, heal, and solve all of our problems and pains. Unfortunately, there is more to that truth. Healing takes prayer, persistence, and more power than most people tend to understand. It's oftentimes more uncomfortable to heal from an issue than it was to create or be part of one. That's because we can't heal if we don't deal. We must intentionally and vocally release to God our pains and pasts. We must give God the power to do what only He can do in our lives. We have to choose to uncover, accept, and address the truths within ourselves, our lives, and about our situations. Time heals no wounds, worries, or weaknesses. Only God can heal— in His timing. Time simply changes our perspectives and, hopefully, our level of enlightenment through those experiences.

It not only takes time but also work and obedience to get us through the healing process. It requires us to accept our wounds and also release ourselves from mindsets, environments, and people who inflict them. The process is difficult. If it were easy, more people would free themselves from their struggles, shame, and strongholds.

We're going to pray about it, cry about it, give it to God 26,291,518 times and then take it out of His hands— again. We're likely going to dream about it, make up scenes in our heads of how our lives and situations should have played out, and then condemn ourselves because we can't seem to shake it. As frustrating, debilitating, and exhausting as that may be, God has a lesson in that part as well.

Although we may only see what looks like a continuous failing at letting go and letting God, He also sees our motives. He sees us wholeheartedly trying. He sees that though we are struggling and falling, we are still getting up, talking to Him, and trying again. It's in those times that every little step we make to follow Jesus, no matter how slow or shaky, is building our trust and relationship with Him. Even in our failure, God is constantly providing us with miraculous strength to continue the path He has created for us. He wants us to completely hand over our cares to Him, but it's our choice to make.

Praying and putting something in God's hands is easy. Completely trusting, letting it go, and keeping it in God's hands... *not so much*. Sometimes, it's our need to control, uncomfortable circumstances, or even desperation for healing that causes us to try to fight battles that are not ours to fight. We want to release pains, people, opinions, and problems, but the process of completely detaching adds an immense fear to what we're already feeling.

Have you ever felt that you knew the right thing to do was hand it over to God, but in the back of your mind, you questioned it? I've been there, too.

That's when we need to remind ourselves that only God can do the best with our worst. He hasn't failed us yet, and He will not start now. God knows what we need even when we think we know better. He can change the course of our lives, situations, and storms in a split second. He can make a mess a masterpiece *if* we let Him. Therefore, let it go, and listen for His instruction. Silence your mind; He will work it out.

It's not uncommon to struggle to see beyond our current situations or feel entangled with the pains of the past. Luckily for us, those tactics of distraction that the enemy sends to destroy us mentally, spiritually, and physically can be used to develop our awareness, maturity, and spiritual strength.

THE PURGING

For years, I hindered my healing because instead of assessing and addressing the source of my ails, I tried to soothe the pain of the exterior with "remedies" that only made the wounds deeper. I was the most "put together" human—who was falling apart.

If you're anything like me, the journey of releasing control—and sometimes even accepting the chaos—was difficult. My issue was not hearing direction and confirmation. It was heeding wise counsel and letting God do what He needed to do.

Everyone talks about the beauty of growth, yet the world often shies away from discussing the uncomfortable truth of mourning one's past self, relationships, routines, or conditions. I can remember sitting on my psychologist's couch crying and telling him that I was mourning the death of myself. That was the best way I could describe everything I was feeling. Nothing felt safe or clear anymore. I didn't know what tomorrow would bring, but I knew I couldn't take the burdens of my negative emotions, pains, or past mindset with me. I had to let go of it all. It was excruciating at times, but feeling the pain was necessary.

Before I could detox and redirect, I had to dive into it, identify it, and express it so that I could heal from it. Purging is painful, but it is also a critical part of the healing and growing process. I couldn't hold onto who I was and become the person I needed to be. I couldn't hold onto times, words, and situations that could not be undone. I had to choose. I had to let my former life, views, and self go.

We have to let go of how things once were, so we can align ourselves with a life that God wants for us, and sometimes that process may seem unbearable. Healing and dealing with the loss of the people we once were is not only strange, excruciating, and depressing, but also a much needed experience. It's painful yet profound.

I wanted a new life and a fresh start, yet I fought tooth and nail to hold onto the person I once was. I outgrew and no longer identified with the person I was, but I hated the idea of being outside my comfort zone even more. I hated that I didn't know what was next or who I was supposed to be. I hated the idea of losing control, yet I failed to realize that it was my loss of control and self-love that got me in that pit in the first place.

LET GO OR BE DRAGGED

The additional discomfort and repeated cycles were essentially my fault and choice. God's ultimatum was to let go or be dragged. Do I let go of the toxic mindset or continue to self loathe until I take my life? Do I let go of my people pleasing or be a prisoner of outside opinions for the rest of my life? Do I let go of the flesh and work on my spirit or try fixing things my way and prolong my suffering? Do I let go of my plan or run the risk of never walking in the beauty of God's plan for my life?

More often than not, it's the weight that we carry with us that affects us more than the words, actions, or situations that scarred us in the first place. Whether it's because we've grown attached to our pain, or we have issues with releasing control, letting go requires a level of determination and strength that many people tend to overlook. It's coming to terms with the fact that holding onto hope or the way things have always been can do more damage than stepping back and starting from scratch. It forces us to completely release control, routines, and sometimes relationships, and the thought of that can be terrifying. However, if we continue to hold on to people, thought processes, emotions, and things that are not for our overall good, then we are setting ourselves up for greater issues in the future. We must let go of the idea that just because we've always been a certain way or have done things a certain way that we have to continue on that route. We are always free to let go and let God. No matter what it is, we have to give it to God and be good with whatever He gives or doesn't give us back. Sometimes the greatest blessings are not things that God gives but all that He's willing to take away.

DON'T REGRET DUE TIME DETACHMENT

No matter what people say or how you feel, you did the right thing. Detachment from a mindset, person, trauma, pain, or lifestyle is far more than giving up on someone or something. It's picking yourself up and finally realizing the importance of aligning yourself with better.

I know, at times, it was overwhelming and caused you many tears. I understand it was uncomfortable and made you wonder if it was best to stay as you were. As each step begins to get a little easier, and those fingers slowly release the grip of the weights you've been carrying, you will appreciate the change. Give yourself time to adjust to your new journey. You are no longer carrying dead weight. You are beginning a new life. Be patient as your emotions and environments evolve. Be proud of the strides made and the joys that are to come. There is peace in knowing that God has a plan and knows exactly where you are in this season. You've made room for greater. In due time, you will reap the fruits of your labor. Let go and grow.

The cages we confined ourselves to were always figments of our fears and uncertainties. We are free to learn, grow, and spread our wings at any given time. The door is open, but we must make the choice to go through it.

- Morgan Richard Olivier

CHAPTER 11
GROWTH

The interesting truth about self-love, preservation, and growth is that once you identify your true value and potential, you begin to disassociate with all of the beliefs, people, things, and even places that aren't worth your time, energy, or attention. You begin analyzing and asking yourself questions like "What is this trying to teach me? Is this for the greater good? How can this help or hinder my growth?" Growth takes on a new kind of meaning, and the process of building yourself up is often bittersweet. Of all the tools given, the most confusing and compelling one seems to be an increased level of awareness. Whenever we dive into our awareness, it is then that we see the effect that our influences and environment played on our pasts. We then become even more mindful of how we will better prepare for our presents and futures.

As we grow mentally, spiritually, and emotionally, we will subsequently find ourselves outgrowing much more than anticipated. Whether minor or complex, the people we are becoming will no longer seek to water the routines, influences, attachments, and mindsets we were once accustomed to. Discernment, detoxing, and determination were not only the keys that led to this current stage that we are in but will also be crucial in the process of leveling up to the next.

The rose colored glasses are off, and our eyes are now seeking re-evaluation, truth, healing, and wise counsel. We are quick to evaluate yet slow to entertain. Our peace, progress, and the act of pursuing our purpose takes priority over the opinions and pleasing of others. Our biggest project is ourselves. We seek actualization over acceptance and value over validation.

NOT EVERYONE CAN GO WITH YOU

Sometimes, we have to leave people behind and accept that their season in our lives has come to an end. Be ready because that may not go over too well with everyone. Why? Growth is seemingly impossible to fathom amongst those who have not experienced it for themselves. What we take as a means to progress is oftentimes interpreted as a personal jab or case of being *too good*. Unfortunately, we live in a world that penalizes people who've grown from their mistakes, distanced themselves from negativity, or strayed from things that kept them stagnant. People say "You've changed" as if it's an insult, but they find absolutely nothing wrong with people repeating cycles or maintaining the same perspectives and maturity levels for decades. Even more disheartening is that we do this to ourselves. We hold ourselves back and condemn ourselves about the shortcomings we've already been delivered from. We replay and magnify our trials without accepting that it took our struggles to build our strength.

Do not be guilted into missing out on ascension because you're trying to gain everyone else's acceptance or understanding. You're allowed to leave a friendship, relationship, job, or environment that threatens your growth, inner peace, and mental health. You're allowed to reinvent yourself, update your look, try new things, and pursue a life of passion and purpose. No matter how much you try, how good your intentions may be, and the amount of energy you put forth, you cannot control anyone or anything on Earth but yourself. You can't force wisdom on people who are not ready to receive it. You can help, pray for, and encourage someone to be better, but you can't fix anyone or make them change. For someone to change, he or she has to see a need to change. He or she must want it and work for it. True progression, maturity, and insight can't be gifted to another person. We can support, but we can't supply growth. With that being said, sometimes you have to leave your friends or family members behind.

Not everyone can go where you are going mentally, spiritually, and emotionally, and not everyone wants to. That is their choice. With that being said, you will have to learn to be your own cheerleader, your own counselor, and your own voice of conviction sometimes. There will be many times that you will have to clap for yourself, pray for yourself, motivate yourself, prune yourself, and allow yourself to grow in all aspects of your life no matter how uncomfortable or misunderstood it may be, no matter the backlash or obstacles that may create and no matter what that looks like.

DETACHMENT

Oftentimes, you have to subtract some things from your life to realize just how little they add to it. That is when you will learn that not everything you lose is a loss. If an item, friendship, relationship, belief, or activity is removed from your life, and you experience peace, then you didn't lose. You pruned. As uncomfortable and distracting as it may be, remember that you have to let go of the old to make room for the new. New life and good growth will not spring forth from dead things.

It may take a while to come to peace with all that you have to detach from. You have to think. If someone or something has been a part of your life for an extended period of time, you have to first adjust without them. That person or thing was a piece to your puzzle. Dependent upon what it was, sometimes you don't feel complete without it. In time, that space will be filled, but first there will be a void. You will miss it or them. You will miss the comfort, accessibility, and even routine that came with it. However, as you grow and heal, your perception toward that experience, person, and yourself will change. You will begin to discern the difference between an attachment and a connection. That is the game changer.

Those revelations became very clear to me once I began to accept the fact that not everyone or everything is meant or aligned with me. Some people and even personal outlooks stemmed from attachments, insecurities or conditioning. Some have reached their expiration and need to be done away with. There are people and things I no longer want in my life, not because I hate them or feel superior but because I now love and honor myself to the point that I put my authenticity before acceptance. I refuse to help anyone hurt me. I hold onto peace, not people. I've removed the chain of people-pleasing and saying yes to everyone around me whenever it means saying no to myself.

BOUNDARIES

Boundaries are not about hurting others. In fact, when you get right down to it, boundaries are not about other people at all. They're solely and rightfully about you. They're about protecting your peace, physical well-being, mental health, spiritual journey, and growth. Sometimes, what's best for you is not well received by others, and no one dislikes boundaries more than the people who commonly abuse them: the narcissists, the fakes, and the opportunistic companions.

Be ready for the guilt trip. It's not a matter of *if* they will have a problem. It's *when*. No matter how misunderstood and mean others may try to make you feel, remember your motives. Boundaries are not signs of selfishness. Healthy boundaries are acts of self-love.

Boundaries remind us that we set the tone for our relationships and even conversations. We teach people how to interact with and love us, by showing them what we tolerate. If we don't want to be spoken down to, taken advantage of, or drained— then we must stop accepting that type of treatment. Sometimes, we have put others in their places. There are also times that we must limit contact or cut off communication completely, in an effort to protect our peace. Not wanting to surround ourselves or engage in conversation with people due to our fear or ego is one thing. Not wanting to deal with people due to our boundaries and knowledge of self-worth is another.

Granting a toxic person re-entry into your life after you've put in the hard work and energy to detox yourself, mindset, and environment is like mopping the floor and telling everyone with muddy shoes to walk all over your house. You are the only one who suffers and has to continually clean up the mess you worked so hard to fix. In that situation, the only person you can blame is yourself.

Sometimes, we have to separate ourselves to save ourselves and stop wasting our time on people who will only bring us pain or problems. It doesn't matter how long we've known them, how thick our bloodline is, or if others don't understand. If someone is a threat to our peace or growth, then they must go. Period. Inner freedom affirms that we have nothing to prove to anyone else but so much to protect within ourselves. Sacrificing our peace for the sake of someone else's approval says something about both parties. It reveals that we are not yet in a place to value our boundaries over validation, and it also confirms that the other person does not understand or truly have our best interests at heart.

There's nothing wrong with saying we will no longer associate with that circle, give our time to that organization, or will be at that gathering if it means we have to be around energy that drains ours. Our lives don't change for the better because everyone is in good standing with us or approves of us. Our lives get better whenever we understand that we deserve the love, protection, and patience we've been giving to the wrong people and places. We can be at peace with people and not be in their presence. We can forgive people and not partake in any of their functions. We must know and protect our boundaries.

TRANSFORM YOUR MINDSET

Imagine a mindset where whenever you look back on your life, you don't see losses. You see lessons. You see purpose in every pain and wisdom in every weakness that you had to address. Instead of holding onto guilt, resentment, or blame—you understand that God either sent or allowed every person and experience into your life for a reason. They were all placed along your path, in an effort to get your attention and draw you closer to Him. That way of thinking is evident of mental and spiritual freedom. That is a growth mindset. That is a transformed mind.

It's time to unapologetically adopt a mindset that supports your growth, strives for progress, and protects your peace—a view of life that allows you to see yourself as the free, forgiven, and worthy person that the Creator says you are.

MOTIVATE YOUR MIND

1. **Walk in Your Worth:** Refuse to dull your shine in an effort to keep the comfort of people who are addicted to their own darkness. Refuse to discount your worth just because others fail to appreciate your value. Refuse to water yourself down because you fear the discomfort and transition of your growth. Remember that your happiness, success, and responsibilities lie in your hands.

You have more than potential. You have the power to put your dreams, goals, and purpose into motion. Walk in confidence, and understand that the only thing standing between you and your breakthrough is your willingness to believe in yourself.

2. **Rise Above:** Stop selling yourself short and basing your self-worth on someone else's inability to appreciate your value. Stop dumbing yourself down for people to "understand" your conversation or feel comfortable associating with you. Stop living as a mediocre version of yourself because the fear of failure and rejection tries to convince you that this place in your life is good enough. It's time to start accepting that you will only grow in response to the environments you allow yourself to stay in, and not everyone from yesterday will proceed to your levels of tomorrow. Do you want to grow? Assess yourself, remove your toxic traits and relationships, and focus on your future. Quit playing with your progress, and put in the work—because you were not placed on this Earth to merely survive. You were born to thrive.

3. **Claim Your Truth:** Repeat after me. I refuse to apologize for how I truly feel. I refuse to harp over things I cannot change. I refuse to reject myself so that everyone else can

accept me. I refuse to be stagnant. I refuse to be bound. I refuse to fall out of alignment. I am and always will be good enough, smart enough, and beautiful enough to be great. The world does not need to support that truth because gone are the days that I believe the lies of my negative self-talk or naysayers. I am going to ascend, and I will do so unapologetically. No one has to understand my growth, believe it's real, or even like it. No matter their outlook, they will not stop my progress. Before I jeopardize myself, my mental health, or spiritual growth— I will, without a doubt, let go. I know who I am, and it's time to walk boldly as that person.

FOOTPRINTS IN THE SAND

Growing pains are not limited to children. As we have all come to learn, accepting and walking in our growth can feel like a very lonely process.

Looking back, I realize that God was there the entire time. He was testing my faith, building my trust, and carrying me through more than I could even imagine. I see that God was not only present, but He was also protecting me from things that I was too weak to combat and comprehend. He was building me up in my brokenness and used that time to gain my attention and check the intentions of everyone around me and myself. What I was experiencing was much more than a breakdown. God was pruning and preparing me for my breakthrough. I needed every step to help me grow.

Everything I thought was an unanswered prayer, closed-door, missed opportunity, failed friendship, or setback was God sparing me from more suffering and further problems. His time may not have been what I wanted or understood, but it was definitely what I needed. I once looked at the world with a magnifying glass in such a way that observed and judged from a distance but never experienced. It took my most uncomfortable seasons of growth to make me realize how important experience was. Even if those experiences were not favorable, they were needed.

All experiences hold a unique power of teaching people. However, it is our choice if we allow them to make us bitter or better. Our outlooks, actions, and reactions determine if we will grow from the lessons and apply them.

Therefore, I say to you, "Will you walk into your next chapter with the wisdom you acquired by the lessons you've learned? Will you protect your purpose and peace? Will you discover the importance of yourself and your journey and release all that doesn't support your efforts? Will you close the door to your unmet expectations and everything that has held you back? Will you continue to grow in spite of the pain?"

When you get the choice, always grow through what you go through. That is where your power lies.

MORGAN RICHARD OLIVIER

It was then I realized
that no one in this life
belongs to me.

The only people I can keep
are the ones who truly
want to stay.

-Morgan Richard Olivier

CHAPTER 12
FRIENDS

It is said that real issues expose fake friends, and that couldn't be any more true. Experience a loss, setback, failure, or turmoil, and then look around to see who is there. Notice how many of your friends show up to support you while others just stick around long enough to share the story with others.

Where are those people whose aide I jumped to whenever they were down? Where are those people who always want me to party with them? Where are those family members whose needs and best interests I always put before my own? Where are those people who said they would be there if ever I needed them? *Where* are my people? Who are my people?

My problem, without a doubt, was distinguishing the difference between people who followed, flattered and had fun with me versus the people who were actually for *me*. Instead of trying to be everyone's best friend, I took time and began discerning who my friends actually were. I so badly wanted to be accepted, loved, and validated by those around me. When I started taking the blindfold off and stopped being the person who everyone was accustomed to, I had a rude awakening. It became painstakingly apparent that I was a friend to many, but I had very few.

Some peoples' love and loyalty for me was based on condition rather than connection. It was dependent upon how often they saw me, how much I could offer them, or if they benefited in some way. They loved the idea and impact that my love for them created, yet they were incapable of and lacked the desire to reciprocate any of it for me.

Far too often, we confuse stagnation with support. Surrounding ourselves with people whose seasons in our lives expired years ago does not make us *loyal*. It often makes us foolish. We must ask ourselves which relationships are the results of connection opposed to circumstance. Is this someone I keep around simply because we share a bloodline, or do we share a healthy bond? Is this friendship draining me or encouraging me to develop?

REAL LESSONS AND REAL FRIENDS

I had to learn that not everyone who claimed to be a *ride or die friend* would be with me until the wheels fell off. Some were there for the free trip and perks. Some folks were wonderful whenever everything was good, but were nonexistent or insensitive whenever the bad rolled around. They were always down to ride but never had any intentions to help me push.

I was always the kind of friend to put *my people* before myself. I'd drop my plans whenever they needed me. If they had a milestone, I would celebrate them and be there. If someone broke their hearts, I'd wipe their tears and talk them through it. The idea of them being hurt always hurt me, but I had to learn that not every friend felt the same about me. I was "ride or die" for people who didn't think twice about running me over.

It's sad, but it's often those we would give our last to that are the first ones to celebrate our struggle because, for so long, they were the ones there. Some claim to love us but hate on us every chance they get. It's a reality that we sadly have to realize.

ONE-SIDED RELATIONSHIPS

The interesting thing about one-sided relationships is that they are never more apparent than when you feel you have reached your absolute lowest or loneliest. People will fail you, and you will fail yourself. The pain of being kicked while you're down by one of your people is a feeling that is unique. The pain of feeling forgotten by people you always supported, defended, and cared for is a slap in the face. Dare I say, the pain of outgrowing those people and experiences is sometimes seemingly worse. You will learn to truly love, encourage, and clap for yourself when no one is behind you, and your real friends will be undeniably revealed whenever the fake ones weed themselves out.

I've never lost a true friend. I only discovered who the fake ones were. People will hurt you. Tie your heart, and accept that fact now because I'm not simply talking about the people who you don't like or don't like you. I'm talking about friends you'd fight for and family you'd die for.

I was watering everyone else's happiness, success, and vision, and they didn't have a desire in the world to spare a drop when I was drained and withering away. I was a reservoir for people who refused or didn't find a reason to reciprocate. I wanted them to treat me as I treated them. How could I truly expect or desire someone to give me love, respect, or encouragement when, at their core, they can't offer or apply those same qualities to their own lives or situations? It made no sense that it would happen, and it makes no sense that I would sit around and wait for it.

People can only understand and value you at the level in which they understand and value themselves. It's not that I wasn't spelling out my love, loyalty, or importance to them. It's that they were unable to read the depth of the message I was trying to convey.

BIRDS OF A FEATHER

I used to hate whenever my elders said it, but they were right. The company you keep not only says a lot about you but also gives you an idea of what your future holds. Why, you ask? Because friends influence you whenever you're most impressionable, irrational, and irresponsible. They have the unique power to convict you to do better or condone it when you've done wrong. Crazy as it seems, those reactions to our actions play a powerful role in our growth or stagnancy. They can act as a calming voice of wisdom whenever you need balance or bring chaos to your life by simply existing.

Think about it. If you only associate with people who find joy in gossiping about others, never try to hold themselves accountable for their lives, and base their happiness on only tangible things, how do you think entertaining those conversations and spending extended time in their presence will affect you? Then, imagine a group of people who aim to inspire, motivate, and condition you for greater—people who are already in a season that you are aspiring to go into or working to be in—a group of people that discusses ideas, the lessons they've learned throughout life, and their pursuit of progression. It doesn't take a genius to see how the influence of one group can yield greater results than the other. On this journey, you must accept that some people will only slow you down or try to hold you back. Select your circle wisely. Only real love, connection, and loyalty should move forward with you.

SELECTIVELY SOCIAL

Self-awareness does not make us antisocial or mean. It teaches us that we should not only raise our personal standards but also raise those pertaining to the people we allow into our lives. We become selectively social individuals who no longer tolerate foolishness or make excuses for behavior that we wouldn't excuse within ourselves. We are focused and very protective of our energy, direction, growth, and ourselves. We understand that the company we keep, the music we listen to, the clothes we wear, and the environments we place ourselves in play a critical role in our growth and development. Therefore, we detox and realign as needed without guilt or care if the outside world understands.

Friends who we once tolerated, even though we didn't align with, are now exhausting to be around. We are not interested in hearing about a personal problem that someone purposely brings upon themselves and has been doing so for the last decade. We don't care to know about the latest and most likely incorrect gossip that someone heard and now feels compelled to spread. We do not have the slightest desire to be in environments that force us to feel fake. We'd rather miss out than have

146

meaningless conversations. This doesn't come from a place of judgment. This selective nature stems from a place of wisdom.

If it does not bring us peace, stimulate profits, or align us with our purpose, then we are not for it. We stop living with unnecessary burdens when we stop giving excuses and chances to people who were never *for* us.

I live in peace because I don't have to think twice about anything or anyone. I don't have to think twice about sharing how I'm feeling with someone because the people I choose to surround myself with are *my people*. They have proven to be my wise counsel, true friends, and those who have shown their loyalty and love to me. I trust people to the level they've shown they can be trusted and not an ounce more. I no longer wonder if I'm not good enough for some people. I also refuse to dumb down my message or happiness so that other people understand or feel comfortable with me. I don't question my worth because others fail to realize it. I harbor no hate for anyone in life. I no longer resent people because I hold myself accountable for my life, and I understand that it's okay if sometimes people don't take accountability for theirs. I no longer allow myself to be in the presence of those who will smile to my face when I'm in the room but talk and laugh about me the second I walk out.

We are all at an age where we have jobs, goals, and responsibilities. Who has time to sit around and talk about people? Who has the energy to drag people through their lives whenever they know in their hearts they don't want them to be a part of their future?

I used to care so much about what people thought of me and what they believed about me. I foolishly and anxiously wasted years of my life worrying about opinions and actions of people that I cannot control.

If we are favored people, we don't need to be anyone's favorite person. Let's make that point clear. What we need are people who will pray for our growth on this spiritual journey and provide wise counsel whenever we are tempted to go astray. There are people who say that they love us, and there are people who show their love for us. The key is distinguishing the difference.

I don't need an audience to praise me, like me, compliment me, worry about me, understand me, know my heart, cheer me on, or have my back. I can do those things myself. What I need around me are people who have my best interest at heart, truly love me, and want to see me grow. I want honesty and harmony. I refuse to associate myself with people who refuse to learn lessons, and I do not want anyone in my life who does not take accountability for their own. Some people never change or see the reason to change. That is their choice and their business. With that being said, I also have the choice to not associate with or want those people in my life.

Whenever I made the choice to release myself of childish ignorance, impulsive responses, and immature things—I simultaneously made the choice to remove myself from people and environments that found no problem with that type of foolishness. It was not because I deemed people who were not on the same growth track as horrible people. It was because I knew I couldn't truly rid myself of a demon that I was still associated with.

Just like recovering alcoholics are advised to stay away from people and places that push the consumption of liquor, I needed to stay away from people who had toxic traits and spirits that I worked so hard to understand and overcome. Backsliding does not simply occur because we stop loving Jesus or stop caring about our growth. For many people, it creeps up on them because they return to the environments that God already removed and healed them from. They return to the friendships and relationships that were revealed to be toxic, but memories or loneliness fooled them into believing that this time it would be different. In that situation, we can blame other people and even the devil, but the difference between the beginning of our journey and this point is that we know better. We have suffered our consequences and have seen what God has done for us. Though we have that gut feeling that we shouldn't return to those people, places, and perspectives that we were rescued from, we return.

I refuse to be that person. I refuse to endure the pain, the suffering, the foolishness, and the chaos that ultimately led to my redemption. I am walking in grace, and I do not take it lightly. I'm no longer a hurt person who wants to keep the company of hurt people. I'm a healed person who wants to continue her pursuit of healing, spend time with those who are healed, and give empathy to those actively trying to heal.

If I want you to be in my life, I will make a point to contact you, hang out with you, or at least check up on you, but I am not going to waste a second pursuing anyone or anything that means me no good. I don't believe in wasting people's time—including my own. I do not have time to entertain anyone or anything that is not attached to my purpose or means well. I don't care who you are, what you do, or how long I've known you; if you are not for me, then you will likely not see or hear from me. It's not avoidance, fear, anger or bitterness. It's focus, self-respect, priorities, and maturity.

FRIENDLY FACT

We're not going to be liked and understood by everyone, and we shouldn't. We're not puppets. We are people. We have unique characteristics, talents, and views and have experienced things that other people may not have. The problem is that we try so hard to be accepted by everyone around us that we forget that not everyone and everything is meant for us. Not every crowd is meant to be our crowd.

I was so fixated, hurt, and downright pissed off at the people who had left that I failed to appreciate and thank God for the people who were true to me. My real friends were there for it all: the hills, valleys, and the roads in between. They helped me along my journey and made sure that I was not only on the right course but also in a position where I could continue to move forward.

Friends are people who stick with you, love you, encourage you, and protect you during your weakest times. The people who hear your silence, wipe your tears, and pray for you are the ones that truly love you. It's not how long you've known someone, a bloodline, or comfort zone that makes someone worthy of being in your circle. It's their love, loyalty, and motives that mean the most.

Understand that while we are not letting God close the doors to expired friendships, we are simultaneously blocking our blessings for better friendships to blossom.

Know yourself and your circle, and be selective about everything because once you disrespect your peace, time, boundaries, and growth—the world will, too.

PART IV

HEALING AND HONORING YOURSELF

There is a peace that comes with accepting who you are and knowing who you're not. The world will always try to define you, persuade you, and mold you into its own creation, but you are better than that. It's not what people think of you. It's what you know about yourself.

- Morgan Richard Olivier

CHAPTER 13
KNOW YOUR TRUTH

It's so easy to get discouraged and wrapped up in what the world says to you or about you, but what's imperative is that you truly understand and protect all that you are. Don't let the laughter and lies of your enemies or the low points in your life make you lose sight of what truly matters. You have too big of a purpose to worry about pettiness or unsolicited opinions. Remember who God says you are.

The saying, "Sticks and stones may break my bones, but words will never hurt me" may have worked as a child, but we have all come to learn that words can definitely hurt. It's amazing how boldly, loudly, and foolishly someone can speak judgment, falsities, and even death over another person's life based off of his or her own personal feelings, with no proof of facts. It's amazing how people can confidently, incorrectly, and insensitively spread a story of an event or conversation they didn't witness with their own eyes or hear with their own ears. It's sickening how people can hold mistakes, low points, and pasts over a person who has grown or changed. Without consideration of the source or understanding of the root cause of even the most chaotic events, the world seems to give no care to the well-being, reputation, or reality of the person(s) being discussed.

You can't stop someone from attacking your character, believing slander, or bringing up the past, but you can control how you react to it.

It's very hard to defend or compose yourself when people judge your experiences. They let their imaginations and their own flaws set the stage of your situation, when they truly have no idea. They believe without knowing, spread lies, disrespect others, and engage in gossip without shame or hesitation.

It's enough of a struggle to try to figure ourselves out but to be marked by a version of ourselves that no longer exists or judged by a version of ourselves that never existed feels totally different. No matter if the negatives stated about us are fact or fiction, the weight it adds to us is still difficult because it's natural to want our peers to view us in a positive or new light. We find ourselves in a tug of war between viewing ourselves as the majority sees us compared to the people that we know we are. This brings up an internal argument. Do I fight and prove my worth or stay the course and simply continue working on myself?

Consider five lessons before you lose yourself by trying to prove yourself:

1. **Practice the Pause.** Always reflect before you react. A fool never knows discernment, but a wise person uses their restraint, lessons, and insight as his or her covering and compass. That's why even a loss can still turn around and work in his or her favor. It's not the cards that are dealt that determine the win but how they are played. Proving a point is not worth your peace. Be still, and know that righteousness will prevail. Don't allow those who add no value to your life make you believe that you aren't valuable. Some people are so focused on bringing others down that they fail to realize that it's that mentality that keeps them at the bottom. Don't join them.

2. **Silence speaks volumes, and energy allocation is key.** Not everything and everyone stands worthy of your words or reaction. You don't have to address every lie spoken, sit down with every person who hurts your feelings, or release a social media press release to inform your friends and followers of your current state. Discern if someone or something is worth addressing, accepting, or ignoring, but never entertain or argue with a fool. It only proves that there are two.

3. **We can argue, pour our hearts, and scream all day. However, people only understand things to their level of perception.**

No matter if what you're saying is the right thing, the difficult thing, or necessary thing—sometimes, it's best to sit back, shut up, and seek wise counsel to ensure you're handling it the best way. If something is said at the wrong time, at the wrong place, in the wrong season, or to a person who can't accurately perceive it, then the message will not be received or used to its best ability.

4. **Our growth is always more valuable than glory.** You will stop worrying about the opinions of others when you realize that peace and progress are more powerful than popularity. Not everyone will accept you or your journey. That is okay.

5. **If someone is going to believe, assume, spread, or say anything that is demeaning, inaccurate, or could potentially hurt us— why would we even want that person around us?** Take their actions as revelation, and remove them. Focus on yourself and not everyone and everything around you. At the end of the day, most peoples' opinions are just as irrelevant as they are. Choose to not be offended or distracted. The very last thing you want to do is lose your momentum over the opinions and people who mean nothing to you and do absolutely nothing to foster your growth.

RULES OF RESPONSE

Not everyone is trying to break your heart. Some are trying to crush your spirit, tarnish your reputation, or distract you to the point that you feel destroyed. Narcissists aim to end your source of power whenever they feel attacked or their egos are hurt. That is not a testament of their power. That is proof of their weakness. When push comes to shove, do not push back. Do not give them the attention they so desperately desire, and do not go out of your way to expose them or enlighten others. Instead, learn from them. Grow from their tactics and leave them to deal with their own demons because the best way to win a game against a narcissist is to not play at all.

Not all revelation warrants your reaction. Some people will intentionally push your buttons because they want you to lash out on them. They are powerless, but your attention will give them a platform. Some just want the opportunity to get you out of character, dress up a story, and reveal the *real* provoked you.

Fun Fact: projection loves to play a part in persecuting others. Sometimes, people believe things no matter how false, exaggerated, and ridiculous they may seem because it is something that they could see themselves doing. Sometimes, they believe something because they heard it first and didn't even think twice that there could be another side to that story. Sometimes, they believe it because it's finally a juicy story about someone or something that has been squeaky-clean, and the buzz seems more important than the basis of truth. No matter how frustrating, embarrassing, or damaging that may be, remember that there is a lesson to learn and a truth to be revealed. You will see the true colors of your friends. You will see the friends who go out of their way to make you aware of what people are saying versus the people who are going out of their way to spread a story. You will see the family members who are defending your name versus the ones who are defaming it. Most importantly, it reveals the emotions, demons, perspective, or growth that is within or away from you. How you react speaks volumes about your maturity, trust in God, and view of life.

OH, RUMORS

If God allows everything to happen, shouldn't we believe that there is a greater reason He's allowing this attack of our character to transpire? As upsetting, painful, embarrassing, annoying, and downright pathetic as it can be, oftentimes, God allows lies about us to teach us the truth about Himself, the world around us, and ourselves. Therefore, instead of wallowing in our own pity parties, acting on anger, or seeking revenge—let's seek revelation. The objective is not to react or even respond to rumors. The purpose is to let them reveal your personal weaknesses, people, and positioning to you. How, you ask? Simply be still.

Allow others to be wrong, receive revelation of who is meant to be in your circle, and get your mind right. Let the emotions and words that rage from your movements and mouth reveal the strongholds, soft spots, and lack of maturity that reside within yourself. From there, you can not only access and address your inner demons but also stop giving life to the things and triggers they're feeding on. Let the obvious tactics of the enemy reveal your true friends and family. Do not intercept or even entertain their ignorance. Allow it to show you the motives and moral character of others and yourself.

You know the truth, and God knows the truth. Don't lose your peace by trying to prove your point to anyone else. God doesn't reprimand or reward you on the basis of what people think, believe, or say you do. You're punished or promoted on the actual truth.

We would be lying if we said it didn't hurt. We would be lying if we said there weren't times we wanted to seek revenge by hauling out and hurting someone back. It's okay to cry about it, but we have to carry on and remember that no one and nothing is worth us coming out of alignment. Refuse to come out of character for people whose behavior only brings curses upon themselves, their children, and their grandchildren. Let them misunderstand you, judge you, condemn you, discredit you, and do what they have to do to give their weak flesh a sense of worth. That battle is not for you. There is nothing you can do to destructive people that can destroy them more than how they are going to inevitably destroy themselves. In due time, they will reap what they sow.

WHY WORRY?

I was flustered, enraged, and paralyzed by all things, *perception*. It's nothing I can hold or physically move. I was drained to the point of severe depression by how I felt about myself, my past situations, and current struggle. My inability to influence the opinions of others or open their eyes to my truth seemed to just make it worse. Every minute felt like I was being tormented in a prison that resided within the solitude of my own mind. My fears and insecurities grew whenever my mindset became flooded with what I viewed as worst-case scenarios. "What if people believe that's true about me? What if people look at me differently? What if they never know the truth? What if they never grasp the concept that I had fallen from pride to find my purpose? What if my lessons appear invalid? What if they don't understand?"

The truth is, I had and still have absolutely no control over that. People will believe what they want for a variety of different reasons. I can't make someone approve, understand, or see progress in my journey. I can't make people feel my emotions, comprehend the messages I'm trying to convey, or view me as the spirit I know I am. I can't make people view me as beautiful, intelligent, or great. I can't control anyone's outlook but my own.

In the past, I would have taken matters into my own hands. Needless to say, all that ever did was make situations and myself worse. I had to learn the hard way that many ordeals are not about people or situations because if they were, then the cycles would end whenever we detach. Oftentimes, they are tests of our faith, wisdom, and maturity. I had to learn to protect my peace and maintain my focus while walking in grace and growing from my truth.

I realized that by not trying to control what was going on around me, I was better able to control and cultivate what was within me. What better way to deal with a people-pleasing nature than to let them be wrong? What better way to get your ego under control than to have it crushed? Peoples' feelings about me no longer infringe on the facts that I know about myself because I know better. I know everything I've said or ever failed to say. I know the sins I've committed and the level to which I committed and repented of them. I know the motive behind every action and reaction I've ever taken or failed to take. Who am I to focus on foolishness? I've searched myself. I've done the hard work of understanding my thoughts. I've identified my strongholds and rebuked my own demons. I know who I am and who I am not.

YOUR TRUTH

I've lied, been lied to, and lied on in ways that not only broke my heart but also opened my mental, spiritual, and emotional eyes. Like most people, I've lied to others in an effort to make them feel better and in times that I didn't know or understand the truth. But those are not the lies that have held me back or kept me up at night. It's the lies I told in times of fear, panic, and sheer chaos—that may have seemed to help at the time—but only added trauma and trials in the long run. It's the lies about myself that made me a part of the crowd but made me feel like an outsider amongst them. It's the lies of the enemy that led me to break and struggle to remember that facts outweigh anyone's feelings, including my own. It's the lies I told myself that kept me from seizing opportunities, taking advantage of my talents, and placing boundaries in my life that desperately needed to be set.

It's often the lies about us, within us, and around us that get our attention and awaken the need, desire, and thirst for Truth and *our* truth. For far too long, the pain of owning my truth and the overwhelming thought of being rejected for it taunted me. It was a voice that always knew how to whisper worry and insecurities in my ear at my most vulnerable moments. That voice was the cunning, cowardice, and crippling voice of fear. It was the fear of rejection, fear that I wouldn't be loved, fear that I wouldn't be understood, and fear that I would be judged. I feared that I would never be good enough, valued, or accepted—the fear that people would only mock the truth of my trials and transformation that took place. I know now that as alone as those fears wanted me to feel, there are many other people who have experienced them and tried to escape them as well.

We feel that people will not accept us, love us, or value us if they know the whole truth about us. If they would know about the addictions we had or afflictions we currently deal with, they would not find us worthy of friendship. If they found out about that trauma we endured, they may feel like they have to tiptoe around us for the rest of their lives. If they would know about that bad thing we did or said, then they would think we are bad people—if they knew this and if they knew that. We hold back because we don't want to be hurt, but often it's that lack of open expression and honesty that hurts us more.

As I sit back and see just how much I've learned, lost, and lived to discover—it becomes very clear that every word whether factual or fictitious played a fundamental role in my spiritual, mental, and emotional development. It made me seek and speak truth. The subject matter for my writings, wisdom from my experiences, and revelation of my truest self blossomed in the very mud the world dragged my name through. It took lies to make me seek God's truth and accept and honor the truth about His plan. Forget the lies of what's around you.

Tackle the lie that is really affecting you—the belief that your worth, capability, power, and impact are all dictated by people.

MORGAN RICHARD OLIVIER

Oh, how we bog ourselves down with the things we can't undo, the words of those who hurt us, and the memories of pain that we can never quite shake. What good is resentment or regret if it restricts every new breath that we take?

- Morgan Richard Olivier

CHAPTER 14

FORGIVENESS

My issue was not turning away from an experience, iniquity, or something negative. My problem was spiritually detaching from it. I held onto my suffering, anger, and strife then wondered why I could never feel free. My unforgiving spirit was a stronghold that not only held me captive in my mind but also in my pursuit of happiness, peace, and progression. In order to move forward into my future, I had to stop looking back to the pain of the past. I needed to truly and wholeheartedly forgive people, situations, and traumas. Most importantly, I needed to forgive myself.

There are some things in life that seem unforgivable and too painful to digest. Whether it's something we've done or had done to us, the idea of forgiving and forgetting seems almost impossible. Forgiving is one thing, but for us to forget seems to be a completely different story. Wouldn't it be foolish to forgive and act like nothing has ever happened? After all, isn't that how history repeats itself? Those questions that we ask ourselves seem valid, but there comes a point when we have to search our hearts and ask ourselves if they are coming from a place of ego, entitlement, enlightenment, or empathy?

No one, and I mean no one, likes to be betrayed, forgotten, disregarded, or hurt. I can't imagine many people finding joy in being talked about, disrespected, embarrassed, or singled out, but somehow we all find ourselves in that situation at some point in our lives—a situation that seems to rip out our hearts, toy with our minds, and seemingly crush us to our very core. Unless we have extremely thick skin and an impeccable amount of emotional strength, it is seldom easy to bounce back from it. We take offenses very personally and find ourselves struggling to overcome not only the pain but also every aspect of it.

With the crushing pain always comes crippling questions. How could I not see past the obvious red flags? When did everything change? Why would someone do this to me? How could I do something like that? What is wrong with me to where this is my life? Could I be that stupid that I would allow myself to be this hurt and in this way?

We look back with pity, yet we fail to see how much that pain has taught us. Failed friendships freed us from a future of stagnancy, and that bad situation made us search and dissect the toxicity from ourselves. All of those things that seemed to wreck our plans were used to put us on a better path. If we are going to see what we want to see and harp on some lessons, maybe we should choose not to forget the fact that even the worst people, experiences, and choices taught us something.

Therefore, to forgive and forget does not mean that you lost awareness of a wrong or that whatever happened is okay. It means that you have gained acceptance, understand that holding onto bitterness or condemnation will not undo the past, and want to release the burden. You choose to move forward in freedom while removing the bondage from the other person or yourself. You choose to show mercy today without holding their shortcomings over their heads tomorrow.

When you find yourself in a state of forgiveness and praying for your enemies' healing or your very own, that's when you know you've grown. Pray for their maturity, mental/spiritual health, and overall well-being. Even if you don't see a change in them or even your situation, you can rest assured that in God's time, there will be a profound change in you. Whether this is someone you love, someone you know, someone you can't stand, or even yourself—you realize that the act of forgiveness is not all for everyone else. It is the final step and tool used to free you. It is your Exodus.

Forgiving Those Who've Hurt Us

It was then I realized
it was never about you.
It was me.
I needed to forgive myself.
Not because you were without blame
but because I was a fool
for seeing you as something other
than what you truly are.

- Morgan Richard Olivier

I'm no longer living in the past, so I have to leave it all there. From my childhood to my adult life, there are people, experiences, and losses that I have to make peace with to not only progress on my journey but also to get my power back. I'm not carrying the weight of anyone or anything anymore. I'm deleting the voices of the people who used, abused, and bullied me as a child. I'm surrendering the "friends" who treated me like I was disposable and the family members who made me feel like they couldn't wait for me to fall. I'm removing the people who took advantage of kindness and plotted on my weaknesses. I'm letting go of the times my feelings were disregarded and my support was nonexistent.

Those who I was always there for and defended that didn't care to come through for me are all vindicated. Do I trust, spend time with, or entertain all the people that hurt me? No. I do wish them all growth and insight because there were times I've been like some of them and needed forgiveness. I forgive them because I understand that people change, things happen, and no one is perfect. We're all human.

I have forgiven people who will likely never acknowledge their need to be sorry, openly defended people who have attacked my character in private, and didn't seek revenge against my enemies when the opportunities were clear. It's not because I was unaware of their motives or too weak to fire back. It's because I've gained the strength of integrity and have received mercy at times that I did not deserve it, too.

Sometimes, we get so wrapped up in the actions of others that we forget that we too have been in the wrong. There are times we have chosen manipulation, selfishness, deflection, and lies over honesty, selflessness, accountability, and truth. We have been the bad guy. Who are we to hold someone bound to their iniquities when we were not only delivered from ours but also developed by them? Who are we to pass judgment or hold on to bitterness whenever God and those we have hurt have chosen to let it go and have had mercy on us? If we want mercy, understanding, forgiveness and grace—then we must be willing to offer it to others. Whether these people are our friends, family, or strangers—they are still people, and people are not perfect.

Some people find pride in hurting others, and—for those people—our forgiveness is needed even more. It's not because we fear them but because we don't want our energy to be tied to them. We don't want them to use our pain, fear, and frustration to be their power source. Furthermore, what good is holding onto a hurt from someone who is obviously hurting?

We may never see someone reap what they've sown, and they may never experience the emotions or chaos they put us through. Karma is never about the last laugh. It's about that person learning their lesson and us finding peace and growth with ours.

FORGIVENESS OF SELF

I thought I'd hate you forever, and I'd never see the value of you again. Your actions, emotions, and ignorance hurt me to the core, and your energy was so heavy that my knees would shake anytime I thought of you. How could a person be so lost, so bewildered, so vulnerable, so fragile, and so undone? I didn't even recognize you anymore. I couldn't figure out how to understand, accept, or fix you. I didn't know where or how to begin. In time, I realized that you needed more from me than you ever did before. You needed conviction and care more than inner criticism and condemnation. You needed compassion in the midst of chastisement. You needed authenticity of

174

self over outside acceptance. You needed a love that flowed from the inside out and boundaries that would help you blossom your deepest strength. You needed me to grow into who I am today. The person I was before—with my whole heart and soul—I truly forgive you. I forgive you for your failures, flaws, and foolishness. I forgive you for not obtaining wisdom until you fell and learned from weaknesses. I forgive you for any wrong road you ever took because they all led you to the path you're currently on. I forgive you for trusting the wrong people because their betrayal was an influential gift. I forgive you for the depression, self-loathing, and doubt because, in retrospect, it brought you a deeper purpose for your pain, relationship with God, and empathy that you now boldly share. I forgive you for yesterday because it was you who made me the refined and resilient person I am today.

By far the hardest person I've ever had to forgive was myself.

Everyone stressed the importance of forgiving others and how you are morally obligated to do so, yet everyone overlooked just how imperative it is to forgive yourself. Until you forgive yourself for who you once were, what you once said, or what you once did—you will not be able to walk in the freedom of who you were created to be.

You condemn yourself and struggle to not only let go of all you've done but all that you failed to do. Sometimes, it's just easier to make excuses and forgive those who hurt you. Whether it's because you have more empathy than most, or you simply don't expect much from people, you find understanding and mercy for those who have wronged you, yet you can't seem to extend the olive branch when it comes to yourself. You've forgiven everything and everyone else. Now, it's your turn.

I forgive myself for saying yes to everything and everyone else but always saying no to myself. I forgive myself for the problems I allowed into my life and my blindness to not heeding God's warnings. I forgive myself for the pain I caused others and the selfishness I exhibited. I forgive myself for my own foolish ways and decisions. I forgive myself for not listening to, discovering, and loving the person who I am. Most of all, I forgive myself for not knowing the things I now know.

I forgive myself for my times of rebellion, anger, and iniquity. I forgive myself for the days I put my power in the hands of opinions, people, and tangible things. I forgive myself for the times I almost let my life and purpose slip through my grasp. I forgive myself for any situation where I lashed out and acted out while in my place of darkness. I forgive myself for succumbing to negative self-talk and missing opportunities not based on my lack of capability but for my lack of confidence and direction. I forgive myself for running from the issues that I should have faced head on and for hitting rock bottom before digging deep, fighting my demons, and reaching for God. I forgive myself for not previously having the mindset, heart, and renewed spirit that I have today.

Until I truly forgave myself, I couldn't move forward. No matter how much I was growing and learning, I couldn't truly heal. I couldn't rest, think straight, or meditate because I had so much bitterness, regret, and sadness on my mind. I had to forgive to be free. That not only saved my life, but it also gave me the courage to unapologetically walk into my new one.

FLAWED AND FREE

Everyone on Earth has hurt and been hurt. We've all fallen short, made mistakes, did things in hindsight we wish we didn't, and felt like the victim in a situation. Forgiving others and forgiving ourselves is not always as effortless as it sounds, but I think we can all agree that life is better whenever we aren't carrying burdens, problems of the past, and condemnation around. It doesn't matter if that person hurt you knowingly or unknowingly or if that person is you. Seek forgiveness, show mercy, and extend understanding. Your new life and freedom is up to you.

It's time to release the past from your hands and mind. That weight is no longer yours to carry.

They will never know the mountains you had to climb, the tears you had to cry, and the mindset you had to leave behind to become the person that you are today. Few understand that it was darkness that made you seek the light and isolation that caused you to search yourself for a deeper meaning. You withstood and gained wisdom through the trials and growing pains and even made peace with wrongs in an effort to make your life, soul, and direction right. You not only persevered but gained a mental, spiritual, and emotional power that you never had before. That's the amazing thing about you. You are more than refined. You are resilient. May you never forget that God used your failures to fix your spiritual vision, brokenness to create a miraculous beauty, and struggles to cultivate an undeniable strength. Nothing that you overcame happened to you. It all happened for you. Your battles built a warrior.

- Morgan Richard Olivier

CHAPTER 15
NEW YOU

It is safe to say that in many ways, I lost myself trying to gain the world, the acceptance of my peers, and love of everyone else only to turn around and lose every single one of those things in the journey of learning, loving, and living as my truest self. Knowing that the journey would take so many wrong turns, cause so many sleepless nights, bring so much pain and pressure to my once comfortable chaos-free conditions, I would do it all again. As crazy as it seems, I would have to relive my worst times because they taught me the best lessons. God used every broken piece to create the unique, fabulously flawed, and favored me.

As you transform into this newer, truer version of yourself, you will notice that nothing is or was truly what it seemed. You will become more aware of yourself and better assess your struggles. You will discover that many of your previous worries were not worth your time and react less because you understand that revelation matters more. Where you were once critical, you will offer compassion. Where there was once ignorance, there is now a thirst for enlightenment and empathy.

Unapologetically adopting a mindset that supports your growth, striving for progress, and protecting your peace becomes second nature because you know that your life will not change for the better until you do. There is no longer guilt in growing. You embrace the fact that you are allowed to reinvent yourself and redirect your path whenever you see fit.

NEW LIFE, WHO'S THIS?

Though your name, exterior, and voice may be the same—you have been made a new creature from the inside out. The world has never encountered, experienced, or had the opportunity to even understand this version of you. That's because you are not back. You are new.

Your outlook is different. The conversations you entertain and what you envision for your life is different. Your goals are different. You are less interested in people liking you because you put energy into honestly liking, knowing, and loving your authentic self. You understand that what someone thinks of you is none of your business or concern. It's what you know about yourself that counts.

PICK THIS VERSION OF YOURSELF

Not everyone will accept you, and that's okay. Not everyone will cheer for you, and that's okay. As long as you love, like, appreciate, accept, and encourage yourself—everything will always be okay. Why? Your success, growth, acceptance and ascension will not be keys placed in the pockets of other people. You know your worth, and that empowers you.

I realized my confidence had formed whenever my inner tone and subconscious concerns shifted. I went from obsessing over if people would like me to sleeping in peace, knowing that some people don't and may never like me. I rested in the fact that I would be fine regardless. I know everything pertaining to me is in order. Therefore, if God is with me and for me, then that is more than good enough.

There was a time that I prayed for people to see my value and appreciate all that I was. Now, as I stand here comfortable, confident, and in control of who I truly am—I often want nothing more than for most people to stay out of my way. I simply want to protect my peace, promise, and purpose. For so long, I followed people who were lost and sought direction from those who still haven't found their way. I needed to learn that my path was unique, and only I could figure it out. I had to get my mind, soul, and life in order so that God could order my steps.

My focus is on my faith, family, and future. I don't want to put myself around anything or anyone who drains the positivity and creativity that now flows through me. God improved everything in my life, and I know that the sky's the limit. I went from struggling to find my career and direction to starting my own company and revamping the family business. My husband and I are closer than ever, about to celebrate twelve years together, enjoying life, and building on the foundation that God built. My mind and soul are renewed, and I am at peace with all that concerns me. I use my lessons to give compassion and empathy to others and use my words to empower and educate those with the same struggles I once had.

I now see that all that appeared to be falling apart was actually coming together. All things worked and are still working together for my overall good. I'm stronger, wiser, more empathic, and aware. From the inside out, I am new and improved.

EMBRACE YOUR EVOLUTION

So often, we mark ourselves by what we consider our greatest mistakes, traumas, or worst seasons. We see the beauty and potential of all that we can become, but we are mentally hindered by the memories of who we once were or how we were once treated. We see ourselves through the eyes of those who don't know our hearts or understand the strides we've made, yet we are blind to the fact that none of that matters. It is that outlook and fear that keeps so many of us stuck.

Some people will always judge us on the chapter of our lives they came in on, whether it was a time of depression, rebellion, or anger and that's understandable. We have to remind ourselves that our lives did not stop there, and we can't let ourselves or others keep us in a hole that we no longer fit in. We are free and whole now. Our stories changed and continuously gained more insight, wisdom, and beauty, even if others aren't there to see it unfold, believe, or understand.

You see, not everyone knows this version of you and not everyone should. So, keep it that way. Not everyone will like, understand, or accept you. That's okay. You will be too much and not enough for some people. That's okay. Friendships will expire. That's okay. Your life will go in a different direction, and your priorities will change. That's okay. What's not okay is smothering your passions, purpose, and potential because change is uncomfortable for those around you.

This new you may not be the most accepted by the world or even comfortable at times, but this version of you is the one that is needed in the world—the one who holds himself or herself accountable, listens instead of judges, and uses wisdom as a means to encourage and empower. This version of you is the person who will make others see the transformation that God can make in someone's life no matter what their past may have looked like. This version of you is the bridge between the person you were and the person you were created to be.

Don't hide, discredit, or badger yourself. Don't fear speaking your truth because you don't think others will understand, and don't hide your joy because those around you live in a world that is dim. Be the light and be yourself. You are the only Bible, self help book, or inspiration that someone will ever read. Don't withhold the good stuff.

MORGAN RICHARD OLIVIER

All of my energy is allocated. I do not have the time, energy or desire to make anyone like me. My concern is not the outdated, exaggerated, or altered image of me that you created in your mind. My priority is to love, protect, and preserve all that I am so that I can fulfill all that I was created to do. So, excuse me as I embrace the power that is within me and encourage others to do the same. Because reaching this level of self-love was no easy walk, but every step was worth it.

- Morgan Richard Olivier

CHAPTER 16
SELF-LOVE

The standards we place on our health, mindsets, and direction are signs of not only our personal growth but also our emotional healing. Though often misinterpreted as selfishness amongst those who lack understanding and enlightenment, self-love is truly a form of self-care and awareness.

It's not apologizing for expressing how we feel and putting our spiritual, mental, and emotional well-being before the expectations of others. It's taking steps back from the pressures of life and paying attention to what truly matters. Self-love is preserving our peace, embracing all that we are, and understanding that we are worthy works in progress.

For longer than we should have, we expected so much from ourselves yet accepted so little from others. We gave until we had nothing left but were always ready to offer more. We effortlessly, recklessly, and unconditionally showed love to others because we struggled to wholeheartedly love ourselves. In learning to love ourselves, we discovered the motives behind our madness and the importance of appreciating and honoring our whole selves.

So many of us try to pick and choose what we love or should love about ourselves. We rip ourselves apart as we try to construct an image that highlights the beauty of our strengths but buries the scars of our weaknesses. As wonderful, presentable, and admirable as that image may be—it will always be void if it lacks acceptance and love. To truly love who we are, we cannot hate who we once were. We have to release our enemies, find peace in the experiences that shaped us, and love all that we've learned and lost.

Sometimes, I think about the person I once was, the friends I used to think I couldn't live without, the things I experienced, and the influences I once entertained. I find myself reminiscing not because I miss them but because it serves as a reminder of just how much God changed my life and how far I've come. I catch myself looking back at the things I used to stress over and just shake my head. The power I gave other people, opinions, and my insecurities were beyond ridiculous. I had panic attacks, lost sleep, and made myself physically sick over situations and possibilities that I ultimately had no control over. I remember the days I cried my eyes out because I felt so lost in the world. I was scared that I would be that way forever but even more scared of the unknown of who I was supposed to be.

However, as I learned to let go, forgive, and find my truest self, I realized that it was all part of the process: my flaws, my faults, my strengths, and my lessons. No matter how I felt about my life or myself, every piece of my puzzle was worth acceptance. Every part, no matter how messy or ugly it was, brought beautiful lessons that worked together to transform my outlook and direction.

I appreciate the person I once was, and I am excited about the powerful person that I am. I pray for the purpose-filled person that I am becoming. I say that because I had to realize, understand, and accept that those are three different people with three different experiences and levels of awareness. Mentally, emotionally, and spiritually—each version of myself embodies a different purpose, possesses a different mindset, and represents a different lesson of my growth journey. Where I once saw regret, I now see refinement. That, my friends, is the beauty and point of it all.

Where there is self-love, self-confidence can take form. We understand that our beauty is not based solely on the reflection in the mirror but is reflected in the words we say and the actions we make. It's the endurance and insight someone acquires and applies that shows true strength.

FREE YOURSELF TO BE YOURSELF

Often, the hardest thing to do is be ourselves because, for so long, we believed we needed to be somebody else. We needed to dress, speak, and act a certain way. We needed to fit in because standing out was frowned upon. We buried the beauty of our authentic selves because we were conditioned to conform. Now, at this point in our lives, we realize the journey is our own. It is time to rise above that way of thinking and live our truths. It's time to free ourselves from the pressures of performing and pursue a life of purpose, passion, and inner peace.

You are free to be who you want to be, travel anywhere you want to go, and succeed at anything you put your mind to. You are free to choose who you want in your life and free to release anyone who doesn't see the value of holding onto you. You are free to try new things, make mistakes, and use the experiences to develop your character. You are free to quit anything that steals your serenity and starves your happiness. You are free to escape your comfortable environment to pursue a life of your very own that reflects who you are and who you aspire to be. You are free to be yourself even if that means you are unlike everyone else.

You don't have to have every detail of your entire life planned out today. You just need to begin loving and living your life as it is. Before you can truly love anyone else, you need to love yourself. Before you can truly dive into self-actualization, you must stop drowning in who you are expected to be or who you once were. Your joy, direction, peace, prosperity, impact, and purpose all begin with you.

It's the act of loving and accepting yourself that inspires and encourages others to do the same.

PART V

ALL THINGS WORK TOGETHER

There is something uniquely beautiful about a person who grows from his or her struggles and uses the lessons from their experiences to spread wisdom. It doesn't matter what you've done or how far you fell. Be the example that shows others that they can overcome that mountain, too.

- Morgan Richard Olivier

CHAPTER 17
TESTIMONY

Nowadays, I'm at peace with it all: my life, my family, my circle, my past, my present, and everything pertaining to the direction of my future. I see every person I've ever met, decision I've ever made, and lesson I've ever learned as a necessary step in my ultimate alignment. No one can hurt me with something I've already accepted as part of my testimony. Period. Former things can't hurt me, and future things can't scare me if God, acceptance, and insight are in the midst.

I needed that pain, not for punishment but for the power, perspective, and purpose that I gained. Suffering—as uncomfortable, unbearable, and difficult as it was to experience—taught me the most about the world, God, and myself. It was my greatest pain and most notable teacher that taught me to trust God's promises through the process. I look at life through a blameless and blessed focus. If I did, said, or thought something, then I take my consequences and lessons and make a conscious effort to grow from them.

It's the things that I once regretted that made me reach for God. My life changed whenever I looked back, looked for the blessings, and let go of the bitterness. My purpose became clear whenever my perception of pain changed.

There are lessons and revelations that can only be found in the valleys. There is a unique power in humility that pride will never give. Those trials, tests and triumphs give us testimony, and that is how we overcome them. Accepting and sharing a testimony is like venting to a true friend, going to confession, or crossing the finish line after a strenuous marathon. Once a testimony about a trial, pain, loss, or concern is expressed—the weight is gone. The perception of others is minuscule in comparison to the power that is regained. Everything from our yesterdays—the good, bad, embarrassing, frustrating, and wonderful—were all part of the plan. It's at that very point that it all makes sense that not everything we go through is strictly about us.

Whenever we're going through a hard time, struggling, or suffering from our own iniquities, the very last people we want to hear a speech or word of advice from is a seemingly perfect person. We long for a testimony from someone that's been there and overcame. We want to know that we can get through it and come out better because others have. It's not only comforting and motivational but also profound. It confirms that sometimes the worst times in someone's life can be right before the best times, and that many people find and align with their authentic selves after turning away from being the worst versions of themselves.

We had to go through some things to know some things. We all fight a battle that no one truly can comprehend, but— thankfully—some can relate. It's getting to that point where we can support and share from a place of empathy that makes all the difference. It's spreading the love that we now have available within ourselves.

We shouldn't give up on ourselves or anyone else because things didn't go ideally or because errors have been made. We don't know how the stories end or if the negatives will one day be used for positive. The dark, silent, and turbulent seasons we went through might have been to provide us with the tools and endurance we will need for the next level of our lives. The rebellion, bad decisions, and tragedy our loved one has been experiencing may one day be used as their testimony to counsel another person and show them that they too can come out on the other side. Sometimes, it's the lessons learned from the pit and the hard walks that followed that qualify a person to bring someone else out of their toughest season.

There will come a point where you will make peace with your journey and the routes you've taken. You will appreciate the strength that your past suffering brought you, the wisdom that stemmed from experiences that weakness overtook you, and the grace that was granted in spite of your iniquities. Where we once saw struggles, we will see the birth of our strength. Where we once saw failure, we will see situations that yielded experience and enlightenment. Where we once viewed ourselves as fools, we will begin to accept that it was those lessons that led us to wisdom.

We weren't put on this Earth to be everyone's friend, live life without a hitch, or be perfect. Every betrayal we suffered, every wrong turn we made, and even every tear we cried served a purpose in our life story and has the power to be used in the life of someone else. We all have a story to tell and value that came forth from our trials and triumphs. What better direction can one get than those that come from someone who has already taken the journey?

Without our past struggles, we wouldn't understand the importance of accountability, order, and gratitude or have the empathy to identify with the pain of others. For example, take the various types of pain some of us have had to endure. In the midst of our addictions, we realized that there had to be more to life, and that last high was going to be our final one. It took being locked behind bars to realize that the person holding us back was ourselves, and the prison we've spent the most time in resided in our mind. Only in the slums of our marriages did we understand why we were together, the depth of love we shared, and the importance of rebuilding a stronger foundation. It was in the hours of watching our children fight for their lives that we built our trust and realized just how strong God truly is. It was laying our family members to rest that taught us just how fragile and precious life is.

God allows us to fail, get lost, have our feelings hurt, experience loss, falter, and fall to the very bottom because He knows that if we search ourselves and seek Him, that pain will then have the power to propel us.

No matter how ratchet, rough, and once regrettable your testimony may be, it can truly be the tool that leads to someone's redemption and gets his or her mind and soul right. Some people want testimony, and others want tea—but it's important to put your feelings aside and understand the facts. Yes, your testimony will be discredited, judged, rejected, and manipulated by those who are not ready, open, or intended to receive. To those who are aligned for it and need it—it's their saving grace, confirmation, and validation that can lead to their redemption and healing. At that point, it doesn't matter how many people judge your journey or perceive it in a negative light. When you open your mouth and express your truth, there is power.

God has a way of turning brokenness into beauty, messes into masterpieces, and trials into testimonies. I'm a fraction of who I once was but more whole than I've ever been. I'm more than who I claim to be. I'm who I was created to be.

- Morgan Richard Olivier

CHAPTER 18
THE PEARLS OF OUR PAIN

Pain is precious, has purpose, and can propel you in the right direction if you learn from it and use it. Like pearls, butterflies, and diamonds—God uses darkness, pain, and pressure to produce the most prized and precious works of art. He takes what seems like ugly endings to create the most beautiful beginnings. We are just the same. Past issues do not define our current identity. They were used to develop us. Our loss of direction, depression, isolation, redemption, and revival all served a profound purpose. Their intent was not to simply punish us but to protect, propel, and prepare us for the levels, tests, and greatness to come. It's those chapters of our lives that we don't want to read out loud that God uses to tell and create His story. Though the pits, pains, and problems may have been a surprise to us, they were never a surprise to Him. Instead, they were a part of His strategy to not only show His strength but also provide us with ours.

When your pain turns to power, you quit giving energy to burdens and start counting your blessings. You see how each obstacle was an opportunity to grow, and— without trials, triumphs, and tests—you'd have no testimony. You learn to search yourself and your motives while taking accountability for your past, present, and future. You stop becoming distracted and disoriented by the hate, falsities, rejections, and judgments the world spews and begin using them as inspiration because you know that in time every word will be reaped and eaten. You recognize that there is a revelation in every true and seasonal friendship and absorb the lessons that each person who crossed your path provided you. You see roles various people play in your life, just where they stand, and who really matters. You become more grateful for each loved one and hold them that much closer to your heart. Moreover, you have a spirit of graciousness and thankfulness when you see that it was pain that refined you and showed you just who you are, who you're not, and to whom you will always belong. The storms, trials, and tribulations weren't allowed with the intent to end you. They are placed along your path to equip you.

Character, wisdom, integrity, empathy, and enlightenment are seldom cultivated in an environment of ease or in the safety of our comfort zones. They are the byproducts of endurance, suffering, and strength. The truth is, we have to go through some things to know some things. It's not merely the hurt life throws at us or how low into the pit we sink. It's how we handle it all, what we learn, and how we apply those lessons moving forward. We learn firsthand how fragile life truly is, how one decision separates us from a totally different life, how one moment of compassion can change the mental state of a vulnerable person, and even how situations that were designed to destroy someone's reputation can build his or her character. In the end, all that seemed to be undone intertwined to make perfect sense.

Sometimes, you have to experience pain to appreciate joy, foolishness to seek wisdom, and loss to be grateful for all that you have. No matter how painful, trying, confusing, or embarrassing the storm may have felt—you can't forget all that you gained. If you learned, grew, and overcame—then it wasn't in vain. What the devil intended for harm, God used for your good.

The journey was not always smooth, but the progress I made and the increased level of perception I gained was beyond necessary and needed so that I could become the person who I am today. For such a long time, I struggled to see the purpose of God allowing pain in my life. Now that I have grown in faith, I see that once I began to truly connect with God—my life, vision, direction, and purpose became so much clearer. I needed to discover myself and had no true direction until I denied myself. It was not only imperative that I build and believe in myself but also important that I understood the importance of trusting and seeking God first.

The more I grew to understand Him, His word, His wants, and His way—the more I began to understand myself, the world around me, and why He made me so different. He made me look different, process things differently, and grow differently because the gift and purpose He had for me is different. I didn't fit in because He wanted me to stand out. I needed to be different to minister His message and be understood by people who have always felt so deeply but are fearful to express it. I needed to be different to encourage people who failed at living their perfect lives and needed sound encouragement to turn around and keep going in a better direction. He made me uncomfortable because He knew that's what I needed to begin my change.

Life is about stepping out of your comfort zones, identifying your toxic traits, and nipping them in the bud. It's about discovering your passions, talents, and strengths and using them to align with your purpose. It's about realizing that life will not always give you what you want, but—with God—you will always have more than enough. It's about humility and growth. It's about appreciation and actualization.

Losing our way was always part of our greater plan, whether we knew it or not. We had to go through the things we did and the decisions we made, both the good and bad, to be where we are today. To have the perception, empathy, and endurance we gained—we had to build from the ground up. It doesn't matter how far we fell. We stepped out of our old ways, crippled mindsets, and turmoil with our chins held high— knowing that the people who walked into the storm are nothing in comparison to the resilient people who walked out.

It was the desire to mend our brokenness that pushed us to evaluate and mend our issues, stumble upon awakening, and open our eyes to alignment. It's our determination to be better and learn from it all that makes us connect the many dots throughout our lifetimes and better connect with others. Years ago, we wouldn't have responded in the ways we do now, offered empathy so effortlessly, or moved in the biggest ways by using the smallest vessels. That new outlook came with our new life in the Spirit.

Therefore, celebrate your growth, love yourself, and appreciate the authority and insight God has given you. Be the person who you needed when you were struggling the most. Spread the love and light of your lessons. Have eyes to see the good in others just as you'd want others to see the good in you. Extend empathy because you know how it feels to be misunderstood, judged, and alone. Offer encouragement because you've seen the power that positivity has on progression and the importance of its impact. Be the person you needed when you were younger. Love deeply, give genuinely, and don't harden your heart trying to protect it. Share the wisdom you gained in the midst of your foolishness, and remember that your lessons have the capability to lead others in the right direction.

Show love because it soothes the soul, heals the hurting, and is greatly needed in this world. Lead others to the spiritual light because it's the only force and foundation that not only takes us out of mental and spiritual darkness but also aligns us with purpose along the way. Give glory to God, and be grateful for how far grace has gotten you. Be the person you were created to be. God didn't save you, strengthen you, and sanctify you for you to sit on your talents and testimony or return to a cycle you've been delivered from. He did it because He has a plan for you. Your journey has only just begun.

Now, it's your turn to lead the lost to His love.